Back to the Jerusalem of the East

The Underground House Church of North Korea

Back to the Jerusalem of the East:
The Underground House Church of North Korea

Scripture quotations are from The Holy Bible, English Standard
Version® (ESV®), copyright © 2001 by Crossway, a publishing ministry
of Good News Publishers. Used by permission. All rights reserved.

Fifth Estate, Post Office Box 116,
Blountsville, AL 35031

First Edition

Cover Design & Layout by Christian

Printed on acid-free paper

Library of Congress Control No: 2011926706

ISBN: 978-1-936533-10-7

Fifth Estate, 2010

For North Korea,
may Christ soon wipe away
every tear from her eyes
(Revelation 21:4)

CONTENTS

FOREWORD

I have always been fascinated by stories of Christian perseverance amidst persecution. There seems to be a "warrior spirit" in the heart of the persecuted that is akin to a soldier in battle. As a former soldier and combat veteran, I understand what drives the persecuted church to stand tall during the days of battle.

One of the greatest revivals in all of Asia took place in what is now referred to as North Korea (officially called the Democratic People's Republic of Korea). Now, over 100 years later, most Westerners think the church in North Korea has been destroyed. Having worked inside one of the most closed countries in the world for years now, I beg to differ. Countless numbers of North Korean refugees have fled the country. Many are believers, even after years of persecution and attempts to destroy Christianity. How can that be?

The answers are found in Scripture. When trouble comes, God emblazes the spirit of the church to stand. A great example of this "warrior spirit" from a Christian perspective can be found in the Bible in II Samuel 23:8-12 in the list of David's mighty men:

These are the names of the mighty men whom David had: Josheb-basshebeth a Tahchemonite; he was chief of the three. He wielded his spear against eight hundred whom he killed at one time.

And next to him among the three mighty men was Eleazar the son of Dodo, son of Ahohi. He was with David when they defied the Philistines who were gathered there for battle, and the men of Israel withdrew.

He rose and struck down the Philistines until his hand was weary, and his hand clung to the sword. And the LORD brought about a great victory that day, and the men returned after him only to strip the slain.

And next to him was Shammah, the son of Agee the Hararite. The Philistines gathered together at Lehi, where there was a plot of ground full of lentils, and the men fled from the Philistines.

But he took his stand in the midst of the plot and defended it and struck down the Philistines, and the LORD worked a great victory.

The first example of a man with a biblical warrior spirit in this list is Eleazar. He literally stood and fought until his muscles became so contracted that his sword was literally stuck in his hand. I have found that many believers living in countries where Christian persecution is common develop this spirit of Eleazar; they are willing to stand until the end and work for God with all their might. In this day and age when most people have the television remote control constantly in their hands, or their eyes glued to Facebook, it is refreshing to find underground Christians in persecuting countries clinging so tightly to the word of God and filled with the spirit that emboldened Eleazar that they are quite literally shaking the gates of hell for the glory of God.

Let us turn our focus on the "warrior spirit and Christianity" to a man named Shammah, who exemplifies the persecuted church. The Bible says that when everyone else had run away, Shammah stood "in the midst." I have found that persecution instills in individuals the confidence needed to take a stand "in the midst," come what may. In today's world, many Christians try to straddle the fence and keep both sides happy. One that is taught to have confidence in God through the school of persecution is much more likely to take a stand in the midst of tragedy, when the non-warriors have turned and run away long ago.

Shammah stood "during the crisis." It is easy to stand when all is well. My fellow Americans face a crisis entirely different from the underground Christians of North Korea. Three out of four Americans do not believe in absolute truth. We teach evolution and wonder why our children act like wild animals. The crisis is deeper than these examples, for it runs deep into the heart of American Christianity.

While America experiences the growth of "megachurches," we are still faced with the fact that 70 % of the mainstream churches have plateaued or are declining. Less than ten percent of all American Christians have ever shared their faith. Tens of thousands of churches in America regularly record giving no baptisms, year after year. Yes, there is a crisis in Christianity in the God-blessed USA. Passive Christianity is the cause. The great need in that country is to instill a little "warrior spirit" in the youth of their community so they will not bend, bow, or budge to the system of this world and can stand firm on the principles of God's Word. This is what persecution has done inside North Korea.

The interesting thing about Shammah was the reason for

which he stood. He was not defending all of Israel, the Holy City, the Ark of the Covenant, or the King. He was fighting to defend a "field full of lentils"; a pea patch! Fighting by himself, when the whole army fled, Shammah defeated the whole Philistine army over a pea patch! Why? Because they were God's peas. We learn from Shammah the biblical concept of the warrior spirit, "If it is God's, it is worth fighting for." The church in North Korea is willing to risk everything simply because it is right to do just that.

South Korea is praying for revival in the North, again. They are praying that God will allow South Korea to take the gospel back to North Korea and be used to start a new revival. Many of my coworkers and I are quite certain the opposite will happen. God has purified the North Korean Church, while Christianity in South Korea has largely become deeply entrenched in materialism and the traditions of men. If God so wills that the two Koreas become one again, I believe God will use the church tried by fire in the north to bring true revival to South Korea's materialistic and self-serving "churchianity."

1

INTRODUCTION

I am not able to share many of the details from my experiences concerning North Korea over the years. Maybe I will never really be able to share them. Too many lives would be put at risk and the life work of many of my dear friends and partners would be destroyed overnight.

Many of the reports that you will read in this book may be a bit graphic for the general reader. I apologize for that and wish that these stories were fictional and not from the pages of North Korea's recent history.

At times it may seem that this book is an attack on the government of North Korea, but nothing could be further from the truth. Our goal is not to attack the North Korean government, but rather to reveal the brutal reality that Christians in North Korea have to endure on a day-to-day basis.

North Korea is often called the "Hermit Kingdom" that exists behind the bamboo curtain. I find the idea of a bamboo curtain laughable. A bamboo curtain would be easy to peek through and could be easily torn down and crossed over. North Korea is more like a concrete kingdom with steel bars and airtight iron vault gates jealously protected by borders with land mines and military bunkers.

Since the communist takeover in the 1950s, the authoritarian regime in North Korea has been ruthlessly destroying every sign of Christianity. Christian churches, literature, and symbols have been burned and destroyed. The persecution of Christians as documented by the UN Human Rights Commission is reminiscent of the days of Ancient Rome when Christians were brutally fed to lions or set on fire and burned alive.

Very few people know anything about North Korea. Even the US State Department admits that its knowledge is limited. This could not have been more obvious than during the North's nuclear weapons tests or the speculation over who would succeed Kim Jong Il, someone whom intelligence agencies around the world did not even know the name or age of despite him being the son of Kim Jong Il.

If you ask most people around the world about the state of the church in North Korea, they will either reply that they do not know or that it doesn't exist except in small social bubbles consisting of expatriates or the elderly.

I personally know Christian missionaries who have worked in North Korea for more than ten years and have never met another Christian believer nor had the opportunity to preach the gospel of Jesus Christ without immediate punishment and expulsion from the country. Many of these missionaries feel that there are Christians in North Korea but cannot prove it. Some even claim that the body of Christian believers only exists in the official churches in the capital city of Pyongyang.

Are there Christians in North Korea? Has Jesus Christ been wiped off of the Korean peninsula north of the 38th parallel? Has the communist regime set the stage for a country that will remain atheist?

Many experts and missionary hopefuls have searched for any signs of Christians. They look for religious books being sold or written. They look for buildings with crosses on top. They look for believers walking around with gold crosses hanging around their necks. They are searching for clergy members in traditional clothing that signify their importance in theological hierarchy. The experts have searched high and low as best they could and many of them have come to the conclusion that the church is dead. Many say that believers are an extinct species in North Korea. Perhaps the only thing Christian about North Korea today is its own glorious history at the turn of the last century.

I hope this book brings you the good news that the church in North Korea is far from dead! It is alive, thriving, and indeed growing! Though the winter may be harsh, though the ground may be frozen, though the wind may blow, the Korean church is like a beautiful winter lily that dares to grow even in the worst conditions.

The North Korean constitution actually grants religious freedom. In fact there are three official state churches in Pyongyang, but the freedom granted in the constitution and the three official state churches are, like most things in North Korea, just parts of a staged performance. These things exist to create a façade that the government has carefully set up as part of their propaganda machinery.

In 2002 at Bongsu Church in Pyongyang, Pastor Chang Sung Bok claimed that there is "no persecution against Christians in Korea. Anyone who wants to become a Christian in North Korea is able to do so of their own free will. In fact there are more than 500 churches in our country today where Christians can freely worship." During this interview between Pastor Chang and BBC, the reporter keenly noted that it was December, arguably the most important month on the Christian calendar, and there were no signs of Christmas celebrations.

Many delegations are able to go into these churches on a regular basis to observe the church services, but all of the delegations have reported that it is impossible to verify the freedom of these churches because interaction and private discussion with the local believers is not possible. It is impossible to know how much of the church services are real worship and how much is choreographed liturgy.

The freedom that the North Koreans claim to give to Christians in the constitution is only true on paper. In reality there is no freedom whatsoever. The US State Department reports that new Christian converts are treated with the most inhumane brutality imaginable and those who might have had contact with foreign missionaries often pay the ultimate price.

In North Korea there is only one god. It is the triune godhead of Kim Il Sung, Kim Jong Il, and the Juche spirit represented by a flame.

According to a US State Department report on Christianity in North Korea released in 2005, it was noted that persecution of Christians in North Korea is reaching levels not seen since the brutal days of the Roman Empire. I think that they were wrong—the Romans did not have electricity or modern technology, which has introduced entirely new and excruciatingly painful methods of torture. A November 2005 article in the National Post reported:

> Relying on eyewitness accounts from 40 recent refugees who fled to South Korea via China, the commission says North Korea has created a reign of terror to crush any religious belief that might challenge the god-like authority of leader Kim Jong Il.

The mere possession of a Bible can bring a death sentence, while attending a secret underground church service can result in gruesome public executions.

One eyewitness told commission investigators he witnessed five Christian church leaders being executed by being run over by a steamroller in front of a crowd of spectators.

In another case, a former policeman described how he was involved in the arrests of 11 church members. Two of them were tortured to death during interrogation, while the others were executed, he said. "Having faith in God is an act of espionage," one North Korean refugee told the U.S. commission's investigators. "Kim Il Sung is a god in North Korea."

"The Kim dynasty is much more than an authoritarian government," the commission report says. "It also holds itself out as the ultimate source of power, virtue, spiritual wisdom and truth for the North Korean people. Heterodoxy and dissent are repressed, quickly and efficiently, with punishments meted out to successive generations of the dissident's family. "This study provides compelling evidence of the systematic denigration of religious life in North Korea and of ongoing abuses of the freedom of thought, conscience and religion or belief," the report adds.

The release of the U.S. report coincides with a UN General Assembly vote yesterday in which member states expressed "serious concern" over human rights violations in North Korea.

The General Assembly's social and humanitarian committee approved a resolution put forward by the European Union raising concerns over the use of torture, public executions and restrictions on freedom of thought and religion. The final vote was 84 to 22, with 62 countries abstaining. South Korea abstained and China voted against.

Today, North Korea is led by a man that is at the center of a personality cult. One of the only ways to really get any information about Kim Jong Il is by watching the official North Korean News reports because Kim Jong Il is not a seasoned traveler and foreign news agencies are not allowed to report on him inside the country. He mostly stays within the borders of his own kingdom except for small excursions across the northern border and he only travels by train. The most absurd and delusional claims about who he is come from the official news agency. For instance, North Korean newspapers have carried stories claiming that North Korean sailors have been saved at sea during terrible storms by simply gathering on the deck and singing songs of praise to Kim Il Sung and Kim Jong Il.

According to North Korean historical literature, Kim Jong Il was born in a log cabin inside a secret base on Korea's most sacred mountain, Mt. Baekdu. At the moment of his birth a bright star lit up the sky, the season instantly changed from winter to spring, and a double rainbow appeared in the sky. This miraculous account seems to be similar to the birth of Jesus Christ and is much more glamorous than the real reports of his birth. These seem to indicate that he was really born in a Russian guerilla training camp while his father was hiding from the Japanese during World War II.

Kim Jong Il has reportedly created a new kind of food. It is called, "double bread with meat" and looks exactly like a hamburger. Despite such evidence, since calling it a hamburger would indicate that Kim Jong Il didn't create it and would be rejected as a capitalistic influence from the West, it remains a double bread with meat.

Even more absurd claims bordering on prepubescent bragging have been made of this god-like leader. In 1994 it was "officially" reported by Pyongyang media outlets that Kim Jong Il shot 38 under par on a regular 18-hole golf course. This included 5 holes in one. More amazing than that is that this was his first time ever playing golf!

When media reporters wanted to come from America to North Korea, Kim insisted that they bring special DVD's of "Desperate Housewives" in order to process their visas (apparently the red leader in 6-inch platform shoes with iron-curled hair is a fan). Kim Jong Il wanted to create a movie industry so he did what any average aspiring director would do: he kidnapped actors, actresses, and filmmakers from other countries and brought them back to North Korea, forcing them to make movies for him. These kidnapped thespians have since left North Korea and Kim now focuses on cartoon production.

Kim Jong Il has one of the largest American movie libraries in the world that no one else in the country can watch, loves jamming with his Ipod that America put an embargo on to punish the leader, and is the world's largest purchaser of Hennessy cognac. He also has short people and handicapped people shipped out of the capital city.

There is very little in North Korea that is real, but what does truly exist is a body of believers in Jesus Christ and their numbers are growing daily. Many people who are familiar with North Korea will challenge some of the facts in this book because they will seem to be unbelievable and those that have had the opportunity to actually live in North Korea will probably be curious because these activities are taking place right under their noses.

There are several well-known Christian organizations that have their sights on North Korea and have been trying to do projects there for years. These groups have indeed pumped millions of dollars into the country in hopes of expanding ministry there. Ask them how many people have come to Christ or how many church leaders they have met with. Ask them how many letters from underground believers they receive on a regular basis. This kind of information is almost unheard of..... almost.

The information in this book is provided by those who are working in North Korea with a completely different focus and methodology. It is provided by those who are working together with the Back to Jerusalem missionaries in China.

Several years ago in 2003, Back to Jerusalem teams contacted many of the Christian groups who were already working in North Korea. Most of the groups on the ground who are able to work inside North Korea are made up of foreigners with Korean ethnicity, like Korean Americans, Korean Canadians, etc. There are also teams made up of the typical Caucasian foreign passport carriers, but they are comparatively fewer in number.

Most of the teams on the ground, representing a collage of ministries from around the world, thought that working with the Back to Jerusalem missionaries from China would be a good idea, but didn't really know how to employ or utilize the young, uneducated, and inexperienced Chinese who typically are from farming areas. In every way, the typical Back to Jerusalem missionary from China looked like a potential waste of resources. Though everyone could see the long term benefit, NO ONE accepted the challenge.

Back to Jerusalem representatives worked with every open network to find platforms for Chinese to get inside North Korea. Chinese came from places all over China to begin studying the Korean language, but were not accepted by the mainstream Christian leaders as qualified candidates for serving in North Korea. These leaders failed to realize that God had a special calling on the lives of these poor, uneducated, inexperienced and unsophisticated Back to Jerusalem missionaries from rural China. How easily we forget that Jesus used a ragtag group mostly made up of fishermen to turn the world upside down and has not ceased to use what is low and despised in the world so that no one can boast in God's presence.

One day it finally happened. Someone on the inside caught the same vision and it developed in a strange way.

It began when Brother Yun first went to South Korea to preach the Gospel several years ago. There were huge attacks that came from the most recognized and established churches and mission groups. Some churches even canceled their meetings with Brother Yun. His autobiography, *The Heavenly Man*, was the number one selling Christian book in South Korea that year and even though there was controversy surrounding Brother Yun, the meetings were packed and the Word of God was preached.

During those meetings there was a young American missionary who had set up a small table and was asking people to help support a project that supplied food to the starving children in North Korea. The leadership asked him to take down his table and to stop handing out brochures because he had not been approved by the local clergy. Something about this young man stood out to Brother Yun and the Back to Jerusalem team. After a quick introduction with the renegade missionary, a vision for North Korea was formed. That American missionary helped pave the way for the first Back to Jerusalem missionary from China to go to North Korea to preach the Gospel.

Working with him, the Chinese missionaries to North Korea have seen many people saved and come to Christ inside North Korea. North Korean pastors have been trained, supplied, and blessed. These simple farmers who were patronized by the elite foreign community suddenly started to do things that others could only dream of. They did not have the financial backing or the know-how, but they had the zeal to preach to their brothers and sisters in North Korea and they had the power of the Holy Spirit upon them to lead and guide their steps.

Suddenly, the Chinese Back to Jerusalem missionaries were in high demand. Many groups began to see the validity and power of partnering with the Chinese underground house churches.

In hindsight, it made perfect sense. North Korea is basically two to three generations behind China. The Chinese have gone through what the North Koreans are going through now. There is a story in American culture that best illustrates the situation.

One day there was a man who fell in a well. He called out for help, but no one was able to hear him. Suddenly there was a businessman who walked by and heard the call of the man in the well. "Dear sir, could you be so kind to help me out of this well," he called. The businessman asked if he had any money and when the man in the well said no, the businessman realized that it made him no gain to help the man in the well.

Then there was a local politician who walked by and heard the man in the well. He told the man in the well to hang on for just a while longer and he would go and form a committee, announce a discussion forum, make a conference call, hold a vote, and return to tell the man in the well the results.

After some time there was a priest who walked by and heard the call of the man in the well. The man called up from the well and said, "Please help, I have fallen in this well and I cannot get out." The priest was deeply moved and replied, "My dear brother. I am deeply moved by your situation, I shall pray for you." Then the priest moved on.

Suddenly there was a tradesman who walked by and noticed the man in the well and was distressed. Without even responding he jumped into the well. The man in the well was perplexed at the tradesman's actions and replied, "Great now we are both in this well and have no way of getting out. What good did you do me?" The tradesman replied, "Yes, but you see, I have been in this well before and I know the way out."

The Chinese have been in the darkness that the North Koreans are currently in. They are actually not all the way out, but they have found the Truth and the Light and they don't want to leave their Korean brothers and sisters behind.

Today when you see Christian groups or agencies in America or Europe talking about taking in supplies to North Korea like humanitarian aid, Bibles, or secret Scriptures printed on the inside of some interesting aid products, sometimes one can almost be certain that the supplies are actually being taken in to North Korea by a Chinese Back to Jerusalem missionary. The group or agency themselves may not even be aware of the fact. It has happened more than once that we have been discussing with groups about "their" secret project in North Korea, only to reveal to them that it was the Chinese who did the project for them without them even knowing.

Korea is a somewhat perplexing place with a leader that is yet to be officially diagnosed as delusional, but unofficially it is generally agreed that he is not normal and runs a country that is shackled in darkness and poverty. Regardless of how hopeless things may seem, today there is a Light being introduced into the darkness and a blessing that is breaking the chains of the impoverished.

More than a half a century ago, before the two Koreas were separated by war and communist ideology, there was a thriving center for the Christian faith: Pyongyang. Pyongyang was then called the "Jerusalem of the East" and it will be so again. This book is about the story of North Korea: past, present, and future.

2

THE ROOTS OF REVIVAL

E ven in the 21st Century it is amazing that North Korea has remained so homogenous. To this day there are no indigenous minority people groups on the Korean peninsula. The Korean people and the Korean language have remained amazingly homogenous. They are said to be related to Manchurians and even today share similar traits. The Korean language is related to Japanese and as amazing as it sounds, is also proven to be related to the Hungarian, Finnish, and Estonian languages.

North Korea was not always a communist country. In fact, it was once recognized as one of the most thriving places of Christianity in all of Asia. Missionaries from all over Asia sent their children to boarding schools in Pyongyang because of the strong missionary influence there.

The Pyongyang Foreign School (also commonly referred to as PYFS) was started in 1900 as a high school for missionary children from China, Korea, and Japan. By the 1930s there were four main missionary schools in Pyongyang catering to the children of missionaries. PYFS was considered to be a strictly Christian fundamentalist school with some of the best teaching in Asia. At that time there were also more than 800 Christian schools for Korean children and together they taught an estimated 41,000 children from various grades.

In the 1930s virtually all western foreigners in Pyongyang were either missionaries or educators with a mission focus. Few business opportunities were of a nature that would lure major investors. PYFS operated for forty years and provided an education for many children whose parents were serving on the Asian mission field.

The majority of the missionaries living in Pyongyang during that time were Presbyterian or Methodist. The mission community had built hospitals, boys and girls dorms, training centers, Soongsil College, vocational centers, and even a Presbyterian theological seminary. All of these buildings stood as a tangible testimony of the missionaries who were ready to make a difference in the lives of North Koreans and share the Gospel of Jesus Christ.

None of those buildings are there today. You can go to the exact location of where these structures once proudly stood but thanks to the accuracy of the US Air Force during the Korean War, none of the structures exist today.

In addition to the more famous PYFS, there were also well-known establishments in Pyongyang founded by Catholics. They were often referred to as the "Maryknollers." They had their establishments across town and away from the Protestants. They did not have a great relationship with the other missionaries in Pyongyang and this was by mutual consent. The Maryknoll territory was known as the Pyong'an Provinces. There were also German Benedictines in Wonsan, Irish Columbans in the Cholla provinces, and French MEP missionaries who were down south in Seoul (some American jokes allude to the French retreating to Seoul even before there was a proper attack). There were even significant records of Seventh Day Adventist activities in North Korea with a hospital in Sunan where the airport now is.

The most in-depth archives currently available on Pyongyang as a mission station are at the Presbyterian Historical Society located at 425 Lombard Street in Philadelphia. The Maryknoll archives can be found in Ossining, New York. Tons of information is available from these archives about the conversions, missionary life and challenges, and projects that took place and how they impacted the lives of the common Koreans. Archives of pictures can also be found there.

One of the reasons that Pyongyang was considered to be the Jerusalem of the East is no doubt due to the number of missionaries who flocked to the city. However, their activities were fueled by the growing number of indigenous converts. It was reported during the 1930s that as many as one out of every five or six Koreans in Pyongyang was a Christian. This figure however is considered to be a conservative estimate and some reports claim there were more. This was a substantial increase in less than half a century.

One of the more well-known citizens of Pyongyang's PYFS was Ruth Bell Graham, the wife of well-known evangelist Billy Graham. Ruth Bell was born and raised in China and her family started a Presbyterian hospital in an area about 300 miles north of Shanghai. Even though there was a Christian boarding school in Shanghai that Ruth could have attended, her parents chose to send her to Pyongyang. Shanghai would have been closer and Ruth would have been familiar with the language and culture of her surroundings, but Pyongyang was where the cream of the crop was. Ruth Bell left for Pyongyang alone to attend boarding school there from the age of 13. She lived and studied in Pyongyang for three years before moving back to America to finish school while her parents were on furlough and eventually attended Wheaton College.

Ruth Bell had the chance to return to North Korea to see the place where she once attended school. When she stood in the place where her school once was she replied to her Korean hosts, "Almost nothing remains from my school days here during the 1930s. But two things have not changed; the beauty of the two rivers that flow through the city of Pyongyang and the warmth and hospitality of the Korean People." During this visit in the 1990s, Ruth was accompanied by two of her children and she spoke of what it was like to be a missionary in Pyongyang sixty years ago. Ruth was also asked to speak at Bongsu Church which was one of three official churches that were open at that time. When she spoke, she recalled the days when Pyongyang was a beacon on a hill for the rest of Asia. "My years in Korea were very important to me spiritually," she recalled. "I pray that each one of you will know, as I discovered during my school days here, that God so loved you that he gave His only begotten son, that if you would believe in Him, you will not perish, but will have everlasting life."

The missionaries who began to create a social bubble in the city of Pyongyang were however, not where the story begins. The story starts long before Pyongyang earned the name "Jerusalem of the East."

Christianity in Korea had one of the craziest starts of any country in the world. Prior to the mid-1800s, there are no real records of Christian missionaries on the Korean Peninsula. However, there are traces of contact with Christianity as far back as 1592. Oddly enough, these first representatives of Christianity (Catholicism) were not Europeans, but Japanese soldiers. In many ways this very statement would make many South Koreans ready to fight. However, the invading Japanese armies of Toyotomi Hideyoshi were converted Christians. One of the top generals in the Japanese invading force was Konishi Yukinaga, a well-known and reputable Roman Catholic. However, his main missional focus, according to historical writings, was to his own men.

In many ways you could say that real conversion in Korea

started from studying abroad. Around 1770, a Korean envoy to China, Chong Tu-won, received a book called "The True Doctrine of the Lord of Heaven." A group of scholars called *Shilhak*, studied the Catholic Literature with hopes of learning more about Western civilization.

In 1783, these scholars asked the son of an ambassador to China if it would be possible to visit Catholic missionaries in China to learn more. Their request was granted and they were sent packing to Beijing where they were promptly introduced to the top priests and baptized! This would seem to be a dream-come-true for any missionary. Instead of going into the dark and lonely areas of the hinterlands looking for seekers, the seekers came from far away countries looking for them. This must have been an answer to prayer for the Catholic missionaries.

When the scholars returned from Beijing in 1784, they were zealous about what they had learned about Western civilization. These scholars began to distribute literature and preach the Gospel of Jesus Christ to anyone who would listen. Contrary to many missionary claims, it was actually the Koreans themselves who initiated and performed the conversion of other Koreans. Concerning Christian history in Korea, Choe Chinyoung in 1972 writes:

> One of the most interesting chapters in the history of Catholicism in Korea concerns its origin. Unlike many other lands, where the Christian religion was first brought by foreign missionaries, in Korea, it began with a kind of "self-study" (self-directed study) of Christian literature by the natives.

It was no small house group that these scholars started. By 1801, there had been more than 10,000 baptisms in Korea.

This explosion of growth was short lived. After the assassination of two prominent leaders in Korea, the newly appointed King Sunjo was left in charge. He was only a toddler at the time, so his mother, the Queen, was the authority in charge and had no tolerance for the newly-converted Christians.

She issued a law that was sent throughout the land demanding that all practitioners of "evil learning" be killed. Over that period of time, more than 300 Christian were recorded to have been martyred and thousands were arrested and brutally beaten, during what later became known as the Shinyu Persecution.

The church was forced underground like they are today to avoid persecution, but their troubles did not stop there. These Christians became known because of the way God blessed their works. Everything that they did seemed to be successful. In the early 1800s all of Korea was experiencing famine on a large scale. This famine seemed to highlight the growing prosperity of the Christian community. Instead of drawing them to Christianity, this only provoked the jealousy of many neighboring Koreans. This jealousy of the Christian community lead to one of the most notorious Christian persecutions: the Ulhae Persecutions. Hundreds of Catholics were targeted and massacred.

Shortly after this persecution, a Chinese missionary by the name of Liu Fangchi left his homeland of China and studied the Korean language so that he could preach the Gospel in Korea. China had a lack of indigenous priests at the time. They needed every clergy member that they could get for the work in China, but Liu felt an unquenchable desire to evangelize among the Koreans. This brave Chinese believer led the way for Catholic missionaries to Korea. This was the beginning of the Back to Jerusalem vision before there even was one!

Are you starting to see a pattern here? The first Christian representatives in Korea were not Western missionaries, they were Japanese soldiers. The first recorded converts were not reached by Western missionaries, but they practically proselytized themselves through self-study of the Scriptures. One of the most notable first missionaries to Korea was Chinese and paved the way for the French missionaries to later follow him.

Korea is definitely a country with a unique Christian heritage. The first Korean priests were sent in the mid 1800s to Macau to study theology and soon after they returned they attended the most common theological seminary known to the body of Christ - persecution. In 1839, a French bishop, two French priests, and hundreds of Catholics were killed in a wave of persecution that swept through Korea.

This wave of persecution did what persecution always does: contributed to the growth of the body of Christ. The father in law of King Ch'oljong (1849-1863) became a Catholic and began to preach the Gospel to his son-in-law. The King became fond of believers and allowed them more freedom. The bishop in Beijing reported to the Vatican in 1857 that there were 15,206 believers in Korea.

Not surprisingly, Satan was not happy. He considered Korea to be his peninsula and launched an all out war against the Church. Of the 15,206 believers reported in 1857, a great wave of persecution started less than 9 years later in 1866. In March of 1866, a French bishop who bravely performed his duties illegally in Korea was detained. The bishop was secretly living in Korea and the authorities didn't even know about it until he became more politically active. In March of 1866 he was publicly executed. That started a wave of persecution where more than 8,000 Catholics were killed.

BUT, such persecution only led to more growth. Soon the Catholic community was so large that in 1877 the official Bible printing press had to be moved from Japan to Seoul to provide for all of the Bibles needed (including the Apocrypha).

Before the close of the 19th century, the Catholics had established schools, hospitals, and orphanages and one of the orphanages had four Korean nuns working at it. These were the first Korean nuns and nothing shows more clearly the establishment of Korean Catholicism as the image of Koreans wearing nun habits.

The first Protestant missionary to Korea was a man from Whales named Robert J. Thomas. At the time of his arrival in 1865, being caught distributing or even receiving Bibles was a crime punishable by decapitation. Not only was Bible distribution illegal, but Korea—at that time called the Hermit Kingdom—didn't even allow foreigners within its borders. Mr. Thomas remained for a few months anyway and began Bible distribution and sales of Chinese Bibles. His next trip to Korea would cost him his life.

As arguably the most believable account of the famous story goes, Thomas accompanied a team of Western and British merchants aboard the armed merchant vessel *General Sherman* as they attempted to start a trade agreement with Korea. On the way up the river toward Pyongyang, Thomas tossed gospel tracts to the Koreans on the shore. Government representatives eventually refused their trade offer and ordered the crew to leave immediately or be killed.

When the tide went out, the ship ran aground, leaving them stranded in hostile territory. The crew fired upon troops sent to apprehend them and a weeks-long standoff ensued. The battle eventually ended when Koreans succeeded in setting the ship on fire, forcing the crew to jump ship only to be hacked to death with machetes on the shore. On September 2nd of the year after his first visit, Mr. Thomas was martyred on the banks of the Daedong River. It is said that the blood of the martyrs is the seed of the church. The seed was truly planted that day. The location of Thomas' slaying would become the heart of the greatest revival Asia had ever seen in 1907. Countless Korean converts would one day be baptized in the same river that ran with his blood.

It is widely believed that Thomas offered his attackers his own Bible, yelling "Jesus! Jesus!" in Korean, but was refused. When the young missionary kneeled down to pray, he was beheaded. His killer was later convinced that he had killed a good man, took the Bible home with him, and years later, his nephew became a graduate from the Union Christian College in Pyongyang and helped revise the Korean Bible.

Shortly after his heroic act, another Protestant missionary arrived on the scene from an odd bedfellow—Japan. His arrival was prompted by the martyrdom of Robert Thomas. The Royal Bible Society of Scotland in Japan sent Nagasaka, a young Japanese missionary, to Korea. He arrived in Busan and distributed Bibles written in Japanese and Chinese as well as tracts from the Gospels written in Korean.

A big shift in the situation in Korea came when an American medical missionary was sent to preach the Gospel in Korea. Medical missions had become a big focus of American missionary societies. Dr. Nelson Bell, the father-in-law of Billy Graham, went from playing baseball to studying medicine in order to go to the mission field. He was reported as jokingly saying, "If you want to be a real missionary, you will become a doctor, because once they are on the table and you are about to perform surgery, the conversion rate is almost 100%." It was never proven that he actually said that, of course, but the joke has some credibility to it.

In 1884, the prince was brutally attacked and almost killed. He had suffered severe sword slashes. A Dr. Allen attended to Prince Min for three months and the prince finally recovered. This single act of Dr. Allen contributed to the trust of the entire royal court. In less than a decade, medical missions was on the rise in Pyongyang. There was a Protestant takeover on the mission field that the Catholics no doubt hated to see. They had been there for years working on the field and now they were being overrun by Protestants. The Presbyterians started a clinic (Northern Branch) in 1884, the Methodists the next year, the Canadian Baptists in 1889, the Church of England in 1890, and the Canadian Presbyterians in 1893. This added to the prominent presence of the Christian body.

Most people are unaware that there was a revival previous to the one in 1907. After the martyrdom of Mr. Thomas, the next year saw seven Koreans become Christians. Not too many, but plants always start from seeds and small sprouts. From these conversions sprang what would later be called the Wonsan Revival Movement. More missionaries arrived from both Presbyterian and Methodist denominations. They were united in their efforts and God poured out His Spirit. Over 10,000 Koreans in Pyongyang alone came to know Christ in 1904. The next couple of years saw over 20,000 more believe on the Lord Jesus Christ for their salvation. And they said, "*Believe in the Lord Jesus, and you will be saved, you and your household.*" (Acts 16:31)

By 1906, the fires of the Wonsan Revival Movement had turned from a blaze to less than an ember. By 1907, Pyongyang had become known as a den of iniquity. Alcohol flowed freely, as did sex. There was even a school that trained women on how to be "ladies of the evening." Here, at the very place where the blood of Mr. Thomas had been shed, in the heart of sinfulness, revival would spring up!

Behold, I am doing a new thing; now it springs forth, do you not perceive it? I will make a way in the wilderness and rivers in the desert. (Isaiah 43:19)

We learn much about this revival from Jonathan Goforth, one of the most prominent missionaries in the history of China, who had been working in Henan Province. He felt called to go to Manchuria to preach the Gospel. He went to the Korean border in Jilin Province and drew crowds of up to 25,000 people per day! He had a real distrust of the Catholics and blamed them for many troubles he had when trying to communicate across the cultural barriers. He felt that many local Chinese and Koreans did not trust him because they assumed that he was a Catholic missionary. There were even times when Goforth was being attacked and his life was in serious danger until he convinced the mobs that he was not a Catholic and that he disliked them almost as much as the mobs themselves. This dislike of Catholics among the common folk largely stemmed from their tendency to meddle in the politics of China and Korea.

One of the events that gives legitimacy to Goforth's claim of the cultural insensitivies causing him problems was when the Catholic church proposed to build a massive cathedral on a site close to both the royal palaces and Chongmyo (a famous shrine built in dedication to the royal ancestors). When the king heard about these plans it was reported that he kindly requested the church to change the location of the site, but the Catholic church adamantly refused. They felt confident that they had the backing of the French government and their close ally Russia. This led to hostility that also affected the Protestant community.

Goforth was known for ministry among the rough and tough men of the Chinese provincial armies. The language he used to describe his feelings toward the Catholic church in Korea was not the typical narrative uttered by missionaries of his day.

Goforth was shaking in his spirit with excitement for the people of Korea. He wrote often about the revivals in Korea and we learn much about the Korean revivals from Jonathon Goforth's famous pamphlet, *When the Spirit's Fire Swept Korea.*

The beginnings of revival were first seen in Korea in 1903. Dr. Hardie, of Gensan, on the east coast, had been asked to prepare some addresses on prayer for a little conference the missionaries proposed to hold. As he was preparing to share from John Chapter 14 and elsewhere, the Holy Spirit taught him many things. When he delivered his talks on prayer all the missionaries were moved. The Korean Christians at the conference were very manifestly moved. Then Dr. Hardie visited ten mission centers throughout Korea and gave his prayer talks. During 1904, ten thousand Koreans turned to God. The revival thus begun continued in power and spiritual result until 1906.

We missionaries returned home to Ping Yang [Pyongyang], humbled. There were over twenty of us in the Methodist and Presbyterian Missions at Ping Yang. We reasoned that since our God poured out greater blessings in Kassia Hills than in Ping Yang, we decided to pray at the noon hour until greater blessing came.

After we had prayed about a month, a brother proposed that we stop the prayer-meeting, saying, "We have prayed about a month, and nothing unusual has come out of it. We are spending a lot of time. I don't think we are justified. Let us go on with our work as usual and each pray at home as we find it convenient." The proposal seemed plausible. However, the majority decided to continue the prayer-meeting, believing that the Lord would not deny Ping Yang what He had granted to Kassia.

They decided to give more time to prayer instead of less. With that view, they changed the hour from twelve to four o'clock. They were then free to pray until suppertime if they wished. Other than prayer, they focused on little else. If anyone had an encouraging item to relate, it was given as they continued in prayer. They prayed for about four months, and they said the result was that all forgot about being Methodists and Presbyterians. They realized that they were all one in the Lord Jesus Christ. That was true church union. It was about being on their knees. It would last. It would glorify the Most High.

About that time, Mr. Swallen, along with Mr. Blair, visited one of the country out-stations. While conducting the service in the usual way, many commenced weeping and confessing their sins. Mr. Swallen said he had never met with anything so strange, and he announced a hymn, hoping to check the wave of emotion which was sweeping over the audience. He tried several times, but in vain. In awe, he realized that Another was managing that meeting and he got as far out of sight as possible. Next morning, he and Mr. Blair returned to the city rejoicing, and told of how God had come to the out-station. All praised God and believed that the time to favor Ping Yang was close at hand.

It was now the first week of January, 1907. They all expected that God would significantly bless them during the week of universal prayer. But when it came to the last day, the eighth day, there was yet no special manifestation of the power of God. That Sabbath evening, about fifteen hundred people were assembled in the Central Presbyterian Church. The heavens over them seemed as brass. Was it possible that God was going to deny the prayed-for outpouring? Then all were startled as Elder Keel, the leading man in the church, stood up and said, "I am an Achan. God can't bless because of me. About a year ago, a friend of mine, when dying, called me to his home and said, 'Elder, I am about to pass away. I want you to manage my affairs. My wife is unable.' I said, 'Rest your heart. I will do it.' I did manage that widow's estate, but I managed to put one hundred dollars of her money into my own pocket. I have hindered God. I am going to give that one hundred dollars back to that widow tomorrow morning."

Instantly, it was realized that the barriers had fallen, and that God, the Holy One, had come. Conviction of sin swept the audience. The service commenced at seven o'clock Sunday evening, and did not end until two o'clock Monday morning, yet during all that time dozens were standing weeping, awaiting their turn to confess. Day after day, the people assembled, and the presence of the Refiner was manifested in His temple. Let man say what he will, these confessions were controlled by a power not human. Either the devil or the Holy Spirit caused them. No divinely enlightened mind can for one instant believe that the devil caused that chief man in the church to confess such a sin. It hindered the Almighty God while it remained covered, and it glorified Him as soon as it was uncovered; and so with rare exceptions, did all the confessions in Korea that year.

What started as the Wonsan Revival in 1903 was later overshadowed by the Pyongyang Revival of 1907. One gentleman, George McCune, said that the outpouring of the Spirit of God on the people and church of Korea was the most empowering presence of the Holy Spirit ever, surpassing even the revivals in Wales and India. From this pouring out that first began at a men's Bible study at the Jangdaehyun Church, the revival spread like a mighty rushing river to all the Pyongyang churches, and then across the Korean peninsula, saturating everything in its path with the deep waters of revival. One missionary said it was the greatest manifestation of the Holy Spirit since the Book of Acts.

Goforth was often attacked by the missionary community. He was a rebel missionary. He often opened up his home and gave guided tours to the locals. He would show the locals how they sleep, how they cook their food on the stove, and how his wife would make clothes and use the dishes to prepare meals. Many missionaries felt that this was intrusive and that the Chinese and Koreans were too dirty and barbaric to invite into their homes. They insisted that it was just a carnival act and they wanted nothing to do with it, but Goforth felt that it was the perfect way to get to know the locals and for them to get to know him. He gave daily tours to groups of up to 50 people a day.

One thing that Goforth taught us about revival is to always understand that it is never the man, the preacher, or the people. It is always the Spirit of the Lord that ignites the fires. Goforth's favorite story to tell was about a woodpecker that was pecking away at a tree during a storm. The woodpecker was working hard to progress on the tree and then suddenly a lightning bolt struck the tree and splintered the tree into a hundred different pieces. The woodpecker flew up without being harmed and swooped down to observe the splintered pieces strewn about on the ground and then replied, "Wow, I am good."

After many chuckles from the audience, Goforth would say that we need to remind ourselves to not be like the foolish woodpecker. We are never the ones who start or sustain the revival. Even though Goforth was at the center of the revival fires, he never credited his abilities, charisma, or perseverance as the reason – it was always focused on the Spirit of God.

As the repeated cycle of persecution, church growth, persecution, church growth continued to hit Korea, it helps us to understand what is taking place. The persecution today in North Korea is nothing new for those who know the history of the country. Just like all of the persecutions prior to the one today, it will be and is being followed by church growth.

3

THE JERUSALEM OF THE EAST

A lthough there were trials, Pyongyang had many good stories to tell. Foreign children were coming in from all over the world and were being introduced to the culture and everyday lives of the Korean people. The rivers running through the city created a wonderful atmosphere for children who were prematurely separated from their parents. The Korean children were also curious about the foreigners and the booming city of Pyongyang provided a great way to get to know other parts of the world through the residents without having to leave the country.

Ruth Bell Graham recalled the cultural exchanges that she had as a little girl. During the cold winters she and her classmates used to go out to the frozen rivers and ice skate. This was such a wonderful time for both foreign and local children alike as they played together on the ice. The trees would bend with the heavy snows of winter and the crisp clean air would fill young Ruth's lungs as she chased after her friends. "Those were some of the most memorable years of my life, and many of my best friends over the years have been people who were classmates there," she recalled. "After leaving in 1937, I never thought I would be able to return."

Many children in Pyongyang were like Ruth and did not

live with their families. The students, faculty, and missionary community at large became their surrogate family. The queen city of Korea had become synonymous with the fastest growing Christian community in all of Asia and some would even say the whole world at that time.

The children of Pyongyang Foreign School would have been taught that the grand city which sat on the majestic bend of the Daedong River was founded during the days of King David by the Chinese Nobleman Kija, whose temple and tomb were among Pyongyang's prime historical sites. The Catholics, Presbyterians, Methodists, and independent missionaries completely dominated the foreign scene in the 1920s and one would not even notice the few Russian merchants, the American Corn Products Company workers across the river, or the lonely Portuguese trader and his family.

Not only did the number of Christians in Pyongyang boast numerical dominance among the foreigners, but the amount and size of the projects they conducted created a type of community competition. It became like a race to see who could build the biggest hospital, the largest school, etc. Just one Presbyterian campus in Pyongyang filled 120 acres in the city center and contained a huge number of institutions. These institutions included Sungsil College (also called Union Christian College) and the Anna Davis Industrial Shops—where Sungsil College Students worked to pay off their tuition. On the same campus was also the Lula Wells Industrial School for vocational training of abandoned wives and widows. Then there were the ever trusty Bible institutes, Theological Seminary, PYFS, Union Christian Hospital, and the West Gate Presbyterian Church. It was an all-inclusive "one stop shop" for all things Christian. A person could be found, saved, healed, educated, ordained, married, and buried all in the same 120-acre plot of land. This is quite astounding, considering the fact that Pyongyang only had a population of less than 180,000 at that time.

Many of the missionaries in Pyongyang at the time had described Pyongyang as being very different than Seoul. It seemed like everyone who lived in Pyongyang lived life with the vision of reaching the people with the gospel. There was a noticeable social aspect that went beyond the walls of the mission compounds. There were fewer distractions and people seemed to want to actively engage in activities with others. Many of the Americans arriving in the early 1900s had experienced revival in their home country and brought that aspect of revival with them.

This doesn't, of course, mean that these missionaries were perfect saints. Indeed they had their issues. Not only were they preaching a rigid gospel that went against many standard practices and pleasures of Korean society - polygamy, smoking, heavy social drinking, and ancestor worship, to name a few, but many of them operated within the strict confines of their denominational practices. Consequently, the majority of Korean converts were automatically subject to church ceremonies and traditions that have nothing to do with the Bible, but were rooted more in Western culture and church history than anything else.

Although the gospel had first come to Korea through her own countrymen, it soon took on a very Western flavor—something that continues to define much of the Korean church to this day. Interestingly enough, when people observe the average Korean worship service today, what they mostly see is the preservation of 19th century Western church practices combined with unnatural attempts to try to recreate the work of the Holy Spirit that took place during the Pyongyang Revival (such as screaming and wailing in communal prayer).

Those missionaries also seemed mainly apathetic to the Japanese invasion and takeover of Korea. Many thought that the more modern governance of the Japanese would equate to more freedom for the Christians. This was but one of many blunders made by the missionaries that lost them the trust of the local people and is still used for anti-Christian propaganda in the North. To be fair though, there was little that they could have done to stop the Japanese takeover.

Another situation that led to many problems was that many of the missionaries forgot that they were missionaries. Rather than serving the people, some of them began to act like plantation owners who made personal servants out of the new converts. Some of the local Koreans resented the Western establishments that were built and never handed over to the locals as was promised from the outset. For instance, Chosen Christian College (later Yonsei University) was supposed to be turned over to local Korean Christians, but the paternalistic missionaries became territorial and protective of their invest-ments. How quickly people forget that ministry is about ex-panding God's Kingdom, not building earthly fiefdoms of hay and straw that will only be consumed before the Judgment Seat of Christ!

Many Koreans were also upset with the indecisive way in which the missionaries responded when the Japanese ordered all school children to participate in Shinto rituals, a form of idol worship. The local Korean Christian community and the foreign missionary community were at odds over how to "render to Caesar what is Caesar's" without denying the faith. When America entered the war with Japan, the American mis-sionaries abruptly returned home, leaving the Koreans to deal with this very divisive issue. This dilemma resulted in a much deeper problem for the Koreans.

The relationship between Japan and their sun goddess can be traced back to an event that took place in 1281. The Mongols had already conquered Korea and had their eyes set on Japan. Japan knew that their chances of surviving a Mongol onslaught were nil, so they made a pact with the devil. The Japanese leader summoned all of the sorcerers of the nation. He was determined to find who the most powerful god was that could provide the Japanese people with protection. The sun goddess was the god that was chosen and the Japanese leader made a promise that if Japan were saved from the destruction of the Mongol army, they would worship her forever. A typhoon sprang up at about that time and destroyed over 4,000 boats and caused an estimated 150,000 casualties. The Japanese named this special typhoon *kamikaze* or "Divine Wind."

From then on, Japanese Emperors who ascended to power needed to ceremoniously enter into spiritual union with this goddess. To celebrate this union, many small shrines, Shinto Shrines, were built throughout the empire. Bowing at the shrine was the Japanese way of rendering homage to the Emperor and the sun god.

In 1937, the Japanese ordered all Christian schools in Pyongyang to participate in this worship of the sun goddess. Rather than submitting, the Presbyterians closed all their schools. However, other denominations rationalized that this was not worship, but being "culturally sensitive." The Japanese saw the success that they had among the Koreans and foreigners and one year later, in 1938, ordered that all church members present themselves to a shrine of the sun goddess before attending church services. It was also ordered that a shrine be built on church property in areas where no shrine existed.

Many Christians continued to rationalize that since the sun goddess was a false god, the practice had no real meaning. The Presbyterians were considered to be the last holdouts and refused to bow, but even among their ranks, they were not united in their stand.

On September 9, 1938 the Presbyterians held a vote - to

bow or not to bow. After many missionaries with other denominations had already decided to take the easy way out of persecution, September 10, 1938 marked the day that darkness reached the Presbyterian Church. Many angry laity had walked out of the meeting before the vote was taken. Under Japanese pressure, the church decided to allow their clergy to bow to the Shinto Shrines. They declared to their congregations that this was not worshiping another god, but was merely being culturally sensitive and performing a civic duty.

The Koreans felt abandoned by the very people who taught them not to participate in ancestor worship or compromise their faith. The very same people who preached to them that serving Christ meant doing away with all idols no matter the cost had compromised at a defining moment for Korean Christianity.

It is easy to see that not everything the missionaries did was right, but despite their imperfections and pitfalls, God was able to use those broken jars of clay to carry His Truth. He used these great men and women of God in spite of their many failures. God was planting a garden in Pyongyang and He had to use something to fertilize the ground with. Though the best fertilizer is stinky, dirty, and has no beauty in itself, the flowers that are fed by it come out smelling sweet and capture the eyes with their stunning beauty. It may not make any logical sense, but this process happens every day and was happening in Pyongyang at the time.

The city was in full bloom. Churches were being built all around the city, hospitals were providing real care for all people and lives were being impacted. There were persecutions and hard times, but in the big picture, there was real tangible progress. Noticeable was improvement in every aspect of life and it was mainly due to the missionaries who had dedicated their lives to preaching the gospel of Jesus Christ abroad and bringing as many people into the gospel life boat as possible.

There are postcards in historical archives that show missionaries handing out tracts in the city. One such postcard shows missionaries lined up on the streets like a well-dressed welcoming committee handing out tracts to every Korean that would pass by. On it you could see local cyclists who had been stopped and were being told everything that they could take in by enthusiastic missionaries who were no doubt using a set monologue they had repeated a thousand times.

Imagine a city so invested with missionary sweat and blood that even the postcards depicted proselytizing as a normal part of city life. Postcards could have surely shown children skating on rivers, local cultural activities, or some monuments of historical significance unique to the city, but it was the missionary endeavors that adequately captured daily life in Pyongyang.

Is it any wonder that Pyongyang was such a powerhouse in the Christian world? Can you imagine what would happen if as many missionaries were to move into Pyongyang today and have no fear of preaching the gospel? What if they were willing to be kicked out or even killed for their calling? Can you imagine the utter transformation that would take place if fear was removed from the missionary community in North Korea today?

In the mid-1800s, missionaries referred to Pyongyang as being "filthy" and full of pagan worship. There was nothing endearing in the eyes of the world about Korea, but there was something about the people of Korea that caught the eye of the Father. The missionaries descended upon this dirty city in large numbers and ruthlessly attacked the strongholds of the enemy. They loved the people of Korea without reservation and this led to a radical revival.

There is undoubtedly a need for tactful ministry in so-called closed countries. There is a need for avoiding confrontation with the law and the powers that be, but to believe that people in closed countries will receive the gospel of Jesus Christ through osmosis is ludicrous. Too many missionaries only exist. Too many missionaries live on the field, go to the grocery store, pay their bills with money lovingly given for God's work, and go about their day in foreign lands without ever making any real contribution to God's Kingdom.

There are missionaries living and working in China and North Korea today that are merely existing. They would have the same impact on the mission field, without the financial drain on their churches, if they would just exist back in their home country. Many missionaries have become so covert and clandestine that God doesn't even know what they are doing.

This is a strange phenomenon for those that are familiar with missions and the mission field. In Asia today, there are literally thousands of missionaries. Anyone who has ever been to Kunming, China or Chiang Mai, Thailand would have a numerical grasp of the numbers. Those two cities have become missionary hubs and these hubs have literally transformed the surrounding communities.

Kunming is the capital city of Yunnan Province. Yunnan has more minority people groups than any other province in China, a feature which has most likely attracted so many mission groups. It is a city that practically sits in the center of a dust bowl. It is often referred to as the city of eternal spring, but that is only an excuse for local building codes to be lax about providing adequate heating and air conditioning.

Practically every foreigner you see walking the streets in Kunming, unless they are a student or tourist, is a missionary of some sort. Even though there are many missionaries and numerous foreign fellowships filled with hundreds of attendees week after week, if you are involved in any project to preach the gospel, you will come across the same few names over and over again.

If you work with conservative Christians, then there is a pool with certain prominent participants who are regularly active. If you work with the charismatics, you will have a different pool, but then the same names of specific individuals come up again. If you work with people who are not involved in either the charismatic or conservative groups, most likely the same names will pop up again. Usually, there are only four or five different people. These are the ones that are not merely existing. These are the ones who have rolled up their sleeves and feel the desperate need for more time to see as many people saved as possible.

There is risk involved in being productive. There is always the risk of being caught in a closed country. There is the risk of prison or expulsion. In some cases there is even the risk of death. There is the real risk of losing hundreds of thousands of dollars invested in special projects, but which is worse—losing a project over attempting to share the gospel or spending the same amount on a project that keeps the gospel a secret from those who need it most?

The missionaries in Pyongyang were almost annoyingly determined and they were on the streets daily sharing the gospel, but here is the thing that most people don't realize: evangelism was technically against the law in Korea! In the late 1800s, most American missionaries arrived in Korea via Seoul under the Treaty of Amity and Commerce between America and Korea. The freedom of the church was not mentioned and thus not legally permitted. This of course forced the missionaries in Pyongyang to be overwhelmingly involved in social work, in fields like education and medicine in order to remain in the country.

Most effective missionaries in Korea held official posts of some sort. They preached the gospel and did it openly. They learned the true "Back to Jerusalem" creed of the Chinese house churches, "It is better to ask for forgiveness than permission when it comes to preaching the gospel."

In 1932, Pyongyang and Korea in general had undergone many changes from 100 years prior. It was a much different place when Charles Gutzlaff of the East India Trade Company first arrived in the summer of 1832. He did not know it then, but he spoke prophetically about the land. Charles was a good friend of Dr. Robert Morrison and believed in doing business as missions. He used trade to build relationships with locals and preach the gospel. Dr. Morrison sent Gutzlaff a large stock of Chinese Scriptures and tracts (which could be read by both the Koreans and Japanese) to hand out during his journeys.

Charles sent a request to the king of Korea to open up commercial trade and had to wait for the reply. While he was waiting, he planted crops, met with the locals, and handed out the Christian material that Dr. Morrison had given him. After a long delay, the answer came that no trade could begin without consent from China. Upon hearing this, Charles prophetically wrote:

At all events it is the work of God, which I frequently commend in my prayers to His gracious care; can the divine truth disseminated in Korea be lost? This I believe not, there will be some fruits in the appointed time of the Lord. In the great plan of the eternal God, there will be a time of merciful visitation for them. While we look for this we ought to be very anxious to hasten its approach, by diffusing the glorious doctrines of the cross by all means and all power...The Scriptures teach us to believe that God can bless even these feeble beginnings. Let us hope that better days will soon dawn for Korea.

Even though Pyongyang was being fondly referred to as the Jerusalem of the East, there were external factors that had to be dealt with. After 1910, Korea was basically being run by the Japanese and they were on the verge of starting a war with the United States by the early 1940s. Even though the Christian community was growing, so was the Japanese intolerance of it. Pyongyang seemed to thrive in such an environment, but the children at the PYFS did get used to seeing things that children in the West do not see.

Across the river from the school was a Japanese airbase. The air squadrons would run their regular drills and do practice bombing using the school yard as their mock target. Soon, America and Japan were at open war with each other and the Americans were forced to leave Pyongyang. Once they left, Pyongyang would never be the same.

After the war ended, some Americans returned to Pyongyang, but the environment was different. Many of the educated elite in the Korean community saw more favor and benefits in communism than Christianity. Soviet and Chinese communists were building their support base on the peninsula and it was only a matter of time before the communists were to take over that half of the country. Americans, especially Christian Americans, soon became public enemy number one. The Korean Christians would have to fight the ensuing battle alone.

Some Korean Christians left the faith altogether. Andrei Lankov, a professor of Asian history in Seoul, was once quoted as saying, "Pretty much every single important Korean Communist of the 1940s came from a Christian family with very few exceptions."

Before the missionaries left, several thousand churches were planted in Korea. Schools, hospitals, roads, clinics, vocational training centers, and small businesses had all been started by the missionaries to help preach the gospel in Korea.

The sick were cared for, orphans were looked after, widows were provided for, the illiterate were taught to read, and love was shown.

Lankov remarked, "It was maybe the greatest success story of the Protestant missionary movement in East Asia." But today the story in Pyongyang is much different. Lankov remarks about current Pyongyang, "It has one of the most repressive policies in regards to religion the world has ever seen. They are worse than Stalin. They are probably as bad as Mao and probably slightly better than Pol Pot."

The *"Jerusalem of the East"* was soon to become the Hades of the East.

4

HERE COME THE REDS, THERE GOES THE CROSS

I n order to understand the persecution that the North Korean church is enduring today, it is important to understand the North Korean government's ideological system and how that system came to be. It was initially communist, but has since turned into a socialist personality cult with a religious flavor.

Communism, of course, is not unique to North Korea, nor was she the first nation to adopt it. Many countries around the world have their own stories of persecution and atrocities brought on by Communism.

The rise of Communism on the Korean peninsula did not begin with the Soviet takeover at the end of World War II. In fact, you could say that it started in the "Jerusalem of the East," Pyongyang—right in the heart of the great missionary center during the 1920's. Communism did not play a large role in politics prior to the Second World War, but it set the stage for the inevitable division of north and south. The left and right groups splintered during this time because of the aristocracy of that era. Upper class Korean officials were pensioned and replaced by the Japanese. The conquerors allowed landlords to retain their holdings so long as they maintained order, often through brutal discipline and heavily taxing the people's rice production. These landowners became entrepreneurs and were constantly finding new ways to exploit their own people to earn more favor with the Japanese and increase their wealth.

The local people were embittered by this injustice and their hatred for the landowners grew. Some Koreans even considered the missionaries to be partly to blame because they had remained silent and indifferent to their struggles. Small groups of younger Koreans became fed up with the injustice of the system and openly defied the imperial government. These militants were soon hunted down by Japanese police. The militants who made it out alive were able to find refuge in China and Russia.

In 1925, the Korean Communist Party (KCP) was set up in Seoul, but most of its members were forced underground due to strong opposition from the Japanese occupiers. Large groups resistant to the Japanese government in Korea began to form. By 1940, there were an estimated 200,000 Korean communist guerrillas fighting against the Japanese. This group was made up of KCP members as well as other secret societies with similar ideology. Among these guerrilla factions was the notorious leader Kim Il Sung, who became an effective and dangerous leader against Japan.

Kim Il Sung stands as one of the most striking figures in North Korean culture today. His people praise him as an omnipotent figure, yet he was also a "son" of the "Jerusalem of the East." He was born Kim Song-Ju in South Pyongan Province on April 15, 1912. His family was neither rich nor poor but heavily influenced by the missionaries of that time. He grew up in a Christian family and would have known the gospel from a young age. His maternal grandfather was a Protestant minister and his father had attended missionary school and was an elder in the Presbyterian Church. Both of his parents were dedicated Christians and taught their children about the love of God. Kim was even well known as an accomplished church organist.

Kim's family was not indifferent to the plight of their fellow Koreans under Japanese rule and oppressive landlords. They reportedly participated in anti-Japanese activities and fled to Manchuria in 1920 to escape famine. It is quite possible that Kim's father put his missionary training to good use while in Manchuria as well. History shows us that the Lord used Japanese oppression to send many thousands of "involuntary" Korean missionaries—fresh from Pyongyang's revival fires—throughout northern China, Russia, and even as far as Uzbekistan, where Korean Christian communities exist to this day.

Less than six years after the trek to China, Kim's father died. The death of Kim's father no doubt had a profound impact on the development of his faith. Any young boy who loses his father at that age is easily susceptible to outside influence, as was the case with Kim Il Sung. While attending middle school in Jilin, China, the seeds of Communist ideology were firmly planted in his mind.

In Kim's autobiography he greatly exaggerates the poverty of his childhood, undoubtedly to win favor with the truly poor people he would rule over. Though not rich, his family was not the poor peasants he described them as. His grandfather provided Christian education to children through a school he founded and Kim went to a school better than most middle class families could afford at the time.

His childhood was filled with a helplessness that turned into rage. Anything that reminded him of the Japanese oppressor drove him into fits of anger. His autobiography also shows his disdain for the American missionaries in Pyongyang who lived like kings while the locals scraped to get by. His hatred for foreigners became deeply rooted in childhood.

In his writings, Kim never alludes to the faith of his father.

His occasional references to "faith" and the "heaven" over Korea are about patriotism, rather than any idea of a supernatural power.

The great many losses Kim experienced growing up undoubtedly led to his disbelief in God. When his father was arrested by the Japanese and dragged out of a class while teaching, Kim noted that the entire Christian community prayed for him with no visible result. How devastating and disappointing it must have been to see a loved one carried away like that, then have prayers for his release not answered. Kim's life was surrounded by oppression, injustice, and the wrongful death of many good people. Rather than prayerfully waiting to see God's sovereign plan unfold, he did what so many have done in similar situations—he turned his back on the Lord forever.

Instead he found comfort in the Communist movement. The communists taught that all men should receive equal pay for equal work and that landowners had no right to get rich on the backs of the poor. The KCP taught that Korea should be free from the occupation of Imperialists. They gave Kim someone to blame for Korea's problems and gave him the comfort of sympathetic comrades-in-arms.

Little did Kim know that his misguided idealism, absent from the God of his fathers, would lead Korea down a road of more poverty, pain, death, and forced slavery than the Japanese would ever inflict.

Later, when recalling his childhood, Kim wrote, "The Japanese colonists used naked military power to suppress the Korean people's aspiration to become free again. The Japanese took away our freedom of press, freedom to hold meetings, freedom to form organizations, and freedom to march. They took away our human rights and properties." Kim wrote this when reflecting on the March First Movement that erupted in 1919. Little did he know then that he too would be guilty of the same atrocities (and much worse) of the enemy that he hated so much.

Kim looked fondly at the March First Movement as a day when the Koreans stood up against the Japanese, but he admitted, "Catholics, Protestants....and other religious leaders .... had planned and executed the March First Movement."

The roots of Communism were being planted in the "Jerusalem of the East" and Kim Il Sung was in the middle of it all. Though many foreign missionaries were accused of being complacent to the oppression of the Korean people, it was the church bells that were used to signal the protests on March 1st. A declaration of independence was read allowed and the marchers shouted, "Long live Korean Independence."

Shortly after the March First Movement, Kim's family moved to China. It was the last time his mother and brother would ever see Korea. Kim enrolled in a Chinese school and became fluent in Chinese, something that proved to be a necessity during his next 25 years in that country. With his true missionary heart and a fake medical diploma forged by a friend, Kim's father started a medical practice that served mostly patients who were too poor to pay.

Beyond medical ministry, his father was also involved in many activities that made him wanted by the Japanese. To keep from being captured, Kim's family had to move again. Since they had no way to move their belongings, a Christian minister named Bang Sa Hyon loaded up his sleigh with all their things and personally pulled it through the snowy terrain all the way to their new home. Unfortunately, this act of Christian love failed to prevent the onslaught that Kim would later impose on countless Korean Christians.

Kim recalled his father preaching sermons to the people and playing the organ. For security reasons, this preaching didn't go on in the standard church building with a cross on top. Instead, they met in a place called Popyong Church, which was actually someone's home. As ironic as it seems, Kim Il Sung's father was a minister in the underground Chinese House Church!

After the death of his father, Kim joined a communist group and was the youngest member. He was soon after arrested at the age of 17 and put in jail for several months. In 1931, Kim was an official member of the Chinese Communist Party and fought 100,000 victorious battles between 1932 and 1945, according to "official" sources. Of course that would mean he had to fight 20 battles per day for 14 years, starting a new battle every hour and sleeping only four hours a night!

Kim's immediate supervisor while fighting for the Chinese army was Wei Zhengmin. Wei reported directly to Kang Sheng who was a high-ranking party member close to Mao Zedong. This connection proved to be vital in years to come. In 1935 Kim took on the name Kim Il Sung meaning "become the sun." Grigory Mekler, a Soviet propagandist, helped prepare Kim for leadership and reported that Kim adopted the name from another Kim Il Sung who had died.

Communist propaganda has done much to exaggerate the achievements of Kim Il Sung, freely altering history when necessary. If he had truly been an undefeated commander, it seems odd that Kim would have to flee to Russia to escape the Japanese, which he did in 1939—six years earlier than North Korean history books report. According to official North Korean accounts, Kim Il Sung single-handedly beat the Japanese out of Korea. However, Kim was missing in action throughout the beginning of the 1940s because he was training in the Soviet Union.

Kim, the only surviving commander in the area, fled to Siberia with the remaining 120 men of his unit. They were forced to join the 88th Special Independent Guerrilla Brigade of the Soviet Army and were assigned to gather intelligence in Manchuria. Before fleeing, his first wife was captured and killed by the Japanese.

While in Russia, Kim met his second wife, Kim Jong Suk who gave birth to a son—Kim Jong Il. Contrary to popular belief in North Korea, he was born on February 16, 1942 in an army training camp in the Siberian city of Khabarovsk.

While in Russia, Kim received his military and political training from the Soviets. In September of 1945 he arrived in Pyongyang aboard the Soviet warship Pukachev. He had been selected by the Far East Command of the Soviet secret police to take charge of forming a new government. When Kim arrived in Pyongyang, he was dressed in the uniform of a Soviet army captain, handpicked by the Soviets to lead a communist government.

Once Kim was Premier, he aggressively engaged the Russians to support his vision to unify Korea and take over the south. He laid out a plan of how he could sweep across the 38th Parallel and re-unify the country in under three weeks. Stalin eventually agreed to his plan and supplied Kim with everything needed to take over the south militarily. No one was planning on UN intervention, let alone having to deal with the full force of the American military.

After US General Douglas MacArthur drove Kim's armies to the Chinese border, the Soviets decided that continued participation would be too costly and abruptly withdrew their support. Kim then turned to his old friend, Mao Zedong. Kim Il Sung's experiences fighting in the Chinese Red Army and his fluency in Chinese were of great help. Mao Zedong had a vast population of young males that was growing too big in his eyes. He needed a good war to help bring those numbers down to a manageable size. The Chinese joined in the fighting en masse and drove the Americans and South Koreans back down to the

38th Parallel, where it all had started.

One of the Chinese soldiers who fought beside the North Koreans was Mao Zedong's firstborn son, Anying. This was the beginning of a blood brother relationship between the two nations. Kim Il Sung had fought for the Chinese and served in the ranks of the Chinese Army and now Mao's firstborn was in the mountains of North Korea fighting with the Koreans.

Mao Anying had joined his unit in Shenyang and volunteered to fight in Korea. He served as a Russian language interpreter in a unit stationed in an area of North Korea with many caves. At around noon on November 25th, 1950, an American bomber dropped four napalm bombs near a cave where Anying was hiding, killing him and two other officers. The death on Korean soil of the son of Communist China's founder truly sealed the bond in blood between the nations.

When Mao was informed of his son's death, he showed how cold and calculated he was as a leader. Mao told the others in the room at the time: "People always die in wars, the Chinese Volunteer People's Army has already contributed many lives, their sacrifice is glorious. Anying was an ordinary soldier, so this should not be considered a big thing just because he was my son."

Mao was infamously emotionless and Kim Il Sung admired him for it.

Once the communists had absolute control of the North, the persecution of the Christians began in earnest. This was the beginning of great suffering for North Korean Christians that continues today.

Upon the recapturing of Pyongyang by communist forces, many local Christian families found themselves in the middle of a country in crisis. The city that was fondly called "The Jerusalem of the East" was quickly slipping into an abyss.

Many Christians fled south as soon as they could. Those

who couldn't make the trek before the border became impassible were forced to face the worst nightmare imaginable. Below is the testimony of one man who made it to the South with his family and would later move to the United States:

When we heard that the Chinese were coming to our aid, we realized our country would soon be in a bloodbath. My family decided we must move south, and in a hurry. We departed for Seoul, but soon heard that the Chinese and northern forces were occupying the area. As we approached the South, my grandfather was shot by U.S. Soldiers who thought he was a spy. [Many defectors were accidentally killed as supposed spies, but suspicions were justified because many spies were also pretending to be defectors.] My mother and I managed to escape and continue south. My grandmother refused to leave, saying she must bury my grandfather in the mountains where his blood had been shed. My father stayed to help my grandmother, my mother's mother, bury my grandfather. He planned to unite with us in Busan. That was 60 years ago. We never heard from my grandmother or father again. I have many relatives still living in North Korea. My brother stayed behind to fight for the North. He was 18 then. He would be 78 if still alive today. I have not seen or heard from my brother in 60 years. My family were devout Christians in North Korea. One of the reasons we chose to flee was the persecution that we had already faced, and the fact we knew it would only get worse after the war. The only member of my family that was not a Christian was my brother. I pray that somehow the gospel made it to him.

My family now resides in the United States, where we are comfortable. I fully support the efforts of the Chinese to take the gospel back to my homeland. I think the only hope North Korea has is the gospel, and the only hope of the gospel getting there is through the Chinese. South Koreans are too busy building big church buildings and making money to reach North Korea. May God bless the efforts of our Chinese brothers and sisters! My family's opportunity to hear the gospel lies within the hands of the Chinese Back to Jerusalem missionaries.

Kim Il Sung moved quickly to solidify his hold on power by instilling fear in the people and purging the ranks of anyone who might challenge his power. He then moved to conduct his first large scale purge, but unlike the great purges that took place in the Soviet Union, the great purge of North Korea didn't even bother using the formalities of a trial. Christians were accused of being counter-revolutionaries, suddenly swept away by the authorities, and simply disappeared with no explanation. They were either executed or sent to work at the growing network of prison camps that few survivors lived to tell about. For this purpose the North Korean Gulag was born.

Churches, Christian schools, and seminaries were raided. Christians were arrested and sent to gulags to be "re-educated." Christian books were piled up and burned. Ministers and pastors were arrested and tortured. North Korea's long night had just begun.

Kim Il Sung had come from generations of preachers and servants of the Lord. Both of his parents had been active in the church. It is shocking to think that they would have been persecuted and possibly killed in their son's new country. The very people that inspired him would have found no place in Kim's new Communist Korea. The brutal dictator was more savage to the Koreans than the Japanese had ever been. Entire families were sent to labor camps. Fear was instilled at every level of society. In Kim Il Sung's mind, the ends justified the means. He felt the Koreans needed a strong paternal figure to help them understand what they didn't know. "If they could only see the world as he saw it," thought Kim, "then the country would work like clockwork and everyone would be equally well-off."

One of the first things that Kim Il Sung did when he returned to Pyongyang was purchase a clock to hang on the wall. It was something his family never had. According to his memoirs, they were too poor to own one, so they would have to go to a neighbor's house to know what time it was and make sure the children weren't late for school. Now he had the chance to not only own a clock, but to run the entire country as if it were one great clock whose internal mechanism needed to be operated by brutal force.

Kim Il Sung embodied the persona of a man who relies on his own strength. Self reliance has come to define the first leader of North Korea and is today touted as the ideology of the entire country, but all mankind seems to have an undeniable, innate, and unexplainable need to worship something.

When God was removed from Pyongyang, Pyongyang started its search for a replacement. It did not have to look far, because in the city lived a man who was eager to fill the void - Kim Il Sung.

The Reds had arrived in full force in North Korea. Backed by China and the Soviet Union, North Korea was well on its way to joining the ranks of the godless nations which attempted to purge Christianity from within their borders. To be a true Communist, atheism is mandatory, thus the first order of business was to eradicate the "opiate of the masses."

Did Kim ever think about the God of his childhood? Did he completely reject the teachings of Jesus Christ? Was he completely given over to the evil desires of his own heart like the pharaoh in the Bible? It was later reported that he admired

Billy Graham. Did he listen to the man whose wife lived and studied in the city that gave his country a new heritage? When he was alone in the quiet of his room during the twilight of his life, did he ever listen to the sermons of the simple preacher from North Carolina? Did he ever regret what he had done? If not, there were at least many others who did.

5

INTO THE DARKNESS: THE YEARS OF SILENCE

Not much is known about the church in North Korea since the 1950s. That is a huge statement worth repeating. Practically nothing is known about the North Korean church since the 1950s.

Imagine the power goes out while you're in the middle of watching your favorite television show. When the television loses power you can't finish watching the program, don't know what will happen next, and desperately want to see how it ends. What's annoying is that the show is still playing, just not on your television set. The show is still being broadcast, but you aren't able to view any of it until the power comes back on.

That is how North Korea is today. The ability to view the "Kim Il Sung/Kim Jong Il Show" has been lost. It is a program that is still on the air, but no one is able to see what is happening. To take the metaphor further, it is a horror movie where the screen has gone black. The horror didn't stop and the atrocities haven't ended, but are in fact empowered by the lack of observation from the outside world.

The previous chapter gave a glimpse into the life of Kim Il Sung. He was the little boy raised in the home of good loving Christian parents. There was a charisma about Kim that drew people to him and could have been used by God, but he gave in to the darkness. He gave in to his hate of the Japanese and the way that they treated his people. He let anger control him, and hated the Japanese for their atrocities.

This hate and anger, mixed with ambition and zeal, created a leader who was easily offended and always suspicious. His relationship with the Chinese and the Soviets changed from day to day, but Kim was determined to make his country self-ruled, self-sufficient, and self-destined. A great darkness had come over the land of North Korea and with it the years of silence.

In the 1950s the world was still recovering from war and the Soviet Union was the world power that everyone watched and feared. North Korea was peripheral at best and wasn't of much interest to most international journalists. After all, it seemed to be little more than a Soviet satellite whose leadership was on the Communist Party payroll. Their "Great Leader" returned to his home country wearing a low-ranking Russian officer uniform and barely able to speak Korean. It was not an image that would have instilled pride in the Korean people.

The country has been referred to by the American CIA as an "intelligence black hole" and most books that talk about the church inside of North Korea are based on secondhand information and speculation. Most of what is known about the church inside North Korea from the mid-1950s on comes from defectors. Some reports have come from people who are able to go inside North Korea, but access for foreigners is very limited. Nationals with foreign contacts are viewed with extreme suspicion as well and structures are put in place to maintain a high level of security.

The communist takeover of the North brought on a massive exodus of Christians to the South. Between 1946 and 1951, it is recorded that 25,000 (or half) of the Catholic population from the North became refugees in the South. The stream continued even after 1952, when 10,000 Catholics fled south with more than 2 million refugees.

Those that did not escape would live through a hell that the world would never fully understand or know about. Many people would be born in such utter darkness and die suffering.

Shin Dong Hyok was one of the people born and raised in that hell. In the dead of winter on November 29, 1996 Shin Dong Hyok was wearing tattered rags that barely covered him from the harsh cold. He was 14 years old, but looked like he was only 10. He sat close to his father who was crying. The North Korean guards forced him to sit in the front row with his shamed father. Shin was scared, but didn't cry. He thought that he was being brought out to the main grounds by the guards to be put to death.

At 14 years old, Shin should have been spending his afternoon studying or outside playing with his friends, but he had none. He was born in 1982 in a concentration camp known simply as Camp No. 14 in Kaechon, North Korea.

As he sat beside his weeping father, Shin soon realized why they had been brought to the front row. His mother and older brother were marched in front of the crowd. They were going to be executed. His mother walked by her little boy and their eyes met for the last time. She couldn't even say goodbye or speak any words of comfort to her son. She was unable to run over one last time and hold the little boy that she had given life to. She was gagged and her hands were bound behind her back. Shin's mother had a noose placed around her neck and was hanged in front of her 14-year-old son, but not before seeing her older son executed by a firing squad.

According to a New York Times report in June of 2007, Shin showed no emotion. He had no love for his mother, nor was he capable of it. He was taught by the government to hate his mother for the crime that she committed. He didn't even know what that crime was.

Shin was a political prisoner by birth and knew no other life. He wasn't educated, loved, or cared for in anyway. Camp No. 14 was the only place in the world that he knew existed. He had never heard of Pyongyang (only 55 miles away), South Korea, China, or America. All he knew was the camp.

Camp No. 15 was close by and is a better known re-education camp. Infamously known as "Yodok," it has even been the subject of a South Korean musical in recent years. Prisoners that go there are "re-educated" and eventually released if they live out their sentence (not an easy feat given that most die within the first three years of imprisonment). Camp No. 14, however, has no "re-education" focus. It is a "Total Control Zone," meaning that those who go in never come out.

The children who are born there are complete slaves. They are beaten and treated in the most inhumane manner. The government doesn't even bother indoctrinating them, teaching them only the skills they need for mining and foresting. They are given just enough food to survive and keep working.

Shin escaped and now lives in Seoul. He was placed in a special shelter that kept him away from the general public for the protection of both. Because of the inhumane way he had been treated throughout his entire life, he was deprived of the ability to show the most basic emotions such as love, sadness, or even the basic idea of being mistreated.

Even Shin's arms are deformed and warped because he was expected to do labor that was far too demanding for his tiny frame when he was only a toddler. The guards at Camp No. 14 have been commanded not to treat the children like humans. As a little child Shin worked twelve hours a day, seven days a week, whether he was sick or not.

Survival in the camps is not likely. They are really just death camps where the government extracts as much labor as it can out of the inmates until they expire. For the North

Korean government it is more productive to work you to death than to simply kill you.

Don't be surprised if stories like Shin's aren't mentioned when you take the Hyundai Asan hiking tour in North Korea (no longer in operation at the time of writing). The editor was very quickly hushed by the panic-stricken South Korean tour guides for even saying the term "North Korean refugee" while on the tour. Those few foreigners who do see the inside of North Korea are usually only allowed in areas where security forces have complete control over what the visitors are allowed to see and participate in.

North Korea is prepared for years of silence, trumpeting only their achievements. The central government tightly controls all media outlets, with television and radio channels playing constant propaganda to shape the minds and thoughts of the people. The anti-religious propaganda is intense and portrays Christians as evil imperialist murderers.

Most Christian exiles who are able to escape North Korea talk about a common show that is called "Choi Haksin's Family." The dramatized North Korean television show depicts a Christian pastor who was ordained during the Japanese occupation and rejects Communism. As a result of his stubborn refusal his mother gets killed, his wife goes insane, his daughter is raped, and his son fights for South Korea and becomes an American spy. The drama makes it clear that Communism is the only choice for someone who loves their family and Christianity is the choice of traitors.

For most North Koreans, these dramas are their only exposure to anything about Christianity or Jesus Christ. These films are meant to combat any potential cracks in the regime's suppression of Christianity.

The government has a growing fear of any Christian growth and sees it as a challenge to their Orwellian state. In

2005, the U.S. Commission of International Religious Freedom produced a document that told the gruesome stories of many North Korean prisoners who were imprisoned for their Christian beliefs.

During the interviews with the U.S. Commission of International Religious Freedom, one former North Korean spoke about a man and his daughter being executed because the family had a Bible secretly hidden in their home. The Bible accidentally fell out of a pile of clothes while she was outside hanging up the laundry. In North Korea, to deter conspiracies and keep family members from doing illegal activities in their homes, the entire family will be punished if one family member is caught breaking the law.

An observer remembers the young girl and her father being forced to an open market area around the Tumen River, close to the border with China. Elementary school students were brought out to watch the public execution. Seven soldiers marched out and shot three shots each into both the father and his daughter. The woman who was outside hanging laundry with the daughter didn't know the book was a Bible. She only knew that it looked suspicious and immediately reported the suspicious activity to the police, as is required by law.

The young girl and her father were guilty of owning a Bible. A BOOK! They were killed for owning a religious book that was written over 2,000 years ago. For owning this old book with stories from another generation, another country, and non-Korean speaking authors, the old man and his daughter were executed as traitors, counter-revolutionaries, and evil conspirators.

The Bible certainly has the power to change lives. The Word of God has the power to free the mind and spirit. The communist atheists would like to claim that they truly free the masses from the "opiate" of religion, but to do so requires forced conformity and severe punishment. Regurgitating speeches and ideology in a robotic fashion is mandatory because it is from Satan. He uses Communism as his vehicle to eliminate Christianity and enslave as many as he can.

According to most mainstream views on eschatology, the gospel must be spread to every tribe and tongue before the end will come (Matthew 24:14). Satan knows that his time is limited. He has to keep the Truth of God's Word from penetrating into the dark corners of the world through whatever devices he can come up with.

Kim Il Sung's parents were Christians for generations. In his own autobiography he talks about the love and kindness Christians showed him, but the God of his parents and grandparents had no place in his new regime.

Kim Il Sung once spoke about the best way to rid a person of their religion, "We could not turn into a Communist Society along with religious people...We learned later that those of religion can do away with their old habits only after they have been killed." He was serious about this. Between 1948 – 1987, it is estimated that Kim Il Sung murdered ten percent of his own population in order to enforce his ideology. Other estimates have placed the number of Christians killed in prison camps during this time to be as high as 700,000. Christians in North Korea's gulags continue to die on a regular basis, even as you read these words.

One soldier tells the U.S. Commission about his memories as a soldier in the North Korean army. He can remember when his unit was dispatched to clear the ground of obstacles so a road between Pyongyang and Nampo could be widened. In 1996, his unit began tearing down a vacant house in Yongkang County that was in the construction zone. When they began to tear down the foundation, they found a small notebook in the debris. Upon inspection, it turned out to contain a list with the names of a pastor, two assistant pastors, and other local Christians.

The contraband was immediately handed over to the authorities. The 25 people who were listed in the notebook were arrested and brought to the road construction site. Five of those detained were listed as leaders and were bound and laid down on the ground. The other 20 were forced to stand on the side. Announcements were quickly made to get other observers to come out and watch. The five Christian leaders lay on the ground while a large steamroller was positioned in front of them. They were told to reject Jesus Christ and serve only Kim Il Sung and his son Kim Jong Il or they would die.

None of the Christian leaders said a word.

They were given another chance to save their lives. These five leaders were told that they could continue living their lives and things would go back to the way that they were if they would only deny the name of Jesus Christ. They were given the same options that Nebuchadnezzar gave Shadrach, Meshach, and Abednego before the flaming furnace and that the Romans gave countless Christians when facing the roaring lions.

The fellow Christians in the crowd began to cry out, begging the leaders to do whatever necessary to save their lives. Their friends and family members could not bear to watch the horrid execution that was about to take place.

The steamroller started up. The ultimatum was offered again: Reject Jesus and live or refuse to deny Him and die. They remained silent. They had made their choice. It was clear that they would rather die than deny the wonderful name of Jesus Christ.

The steamroller began to roll towards the pastor, the assistant pastors, and the elders and drove over their bodies. They were immediately crushed to death. Onlookers said that they could hear the sound of the skulls popping as the steamroller ran over their heads. Some of the Christians who knew the pastor fainted when they saw the crushed bodies. The idea that religion was for fools and made people crazy was solidified in the minds of the soldiers and officials present that day. After all, who in their right mind would sacrifice their life for a mythological person?

In Cape Town, South Africa at the 2010 Lausanne Congress on World Evangelism, there was a young 18-year-old North Korean girl who stood before the crowd. She very simply began to talk about her experiences as the daughter of a senior official in the North Korean government. When he got the first chance to flee the country, he took his wife and six-year-old daughter across the river to China. On the Chinese side of the Tumen River, there are many illegal house churches. Many of them are Korean-Chinese churches that are very sympathetic to the plight of their brothers and sisters in North Korea. They often provide food, shelter, and medicine to the refugees and share the love of Jesus Christ with them.

When Sung Kyung Ju arrived in China with her mother and father, the family was aided by Christians. Her father listened to the gospel of Jesus Christ and became a Christian. It is terribly difficult to understand how hard that must have been for him.

Sung Kyung Ju's father was a government official, meaning that he was not just the recipient of night-and-day propaganda, but was responsible for enforcing and relaying the propaganda. He had been brainwashed since he was a small child and had helped brainwash others. He didn't know of any life other than serving Kim Il Sung and Kim Jong Il, but when he reached China, he found something that changed his life. It wasn't a passport to South Korea (the coveted goal of so many defectors) – it was Jesus Christ.

Leaving the country is often a death sentence if caught. According to U.N. regulations and international treaties that China is a signatory to, China should help provide passage for refugees that flee into their country. On the contrary, China hunts down North Korean refugees like animals and forcibly sends them back to North Korea. The harsh punishment of those that are repatriated is unimaginable. The Chinese that hand over the North Korean escapees know they send them to their deaths, but this does not change their policy at all. There has also been evidence of the Chinese executing North Korean refugees themselves when it was too much bother to repatriate them.

The worst place for Sung Kyung Ju's father to find safety was in China. His best bet was to try and find people who could help him get to Mongolia or Thailand where he would be able to find ways to get his family into South Korea.

Instead, after becoming a Christian her father became deeply moved for the people of his homeland. Suddenly, life was more than just surviving or having a better life in another country... it had true and eternal meaning. Her father began to think about all those Koreans living in darkness north of the 38th parallel; people bombarded with lies every single day of their lives. How will they hear the truth? How will they ever learn about the Savior who gave His life for them so that they could finally be free?

Her father did the unimaginable. In 2006, he went back to North Korea. He didn't go back as a government employee, nor a prisoner, but as a missionary of the Most High God. To return to North Korea as a missionary meant going back the same way that he escaped—in secret, at night.

The mission most likely cost him his life. Sung Kyung Ju never saw her father again. He was caught, imprisoned, and most likely executed.

You would think that Sung Kyung Ju would hate the idea of Jesus Christ. After all, she no longer has a father. The father that she loved and that sacrificed everything for her to have a good life, is now gone because of his love for Jesus Christ. However, she is not angry with her Savior. In fact, she is completely committed to serving Him and is currently in South Korea studying to be a missionary to be sent back to her home country.

It is the dedication of Christians like Sung Kyung Ju and her father who are going to reach people in North Korea. It is missionaries like them that are going to reach into the darkness and break the silence. In 1984, the Far East Economic Review ran a cover story called, "Korea: the Cross and Catalyst." In the review, they paid tribute to the missionaries who had been giving their lives in Korea for 200 years and at that point Korea had seen the canonization of 103 Catholic martyrs, giving Korea more martyrs than any other country except for Italy, France, and Spain.

The blood of the martyrs, both Protestant and Catholic, has been sown on soil that will bring forth fruit. In the South, not only has there been unprecedented church growth, but the pace of their economic growth cannot be compared to their backward brother in the North. Donald Rumsfeld once said that he had a satellite photo of the Korean Peninsula that he kept in his office. The bottom half of the peninsula was lit up like a star at night because of all of the lights in the financially prosperous region and the North was not even visible. Despite the little spot of light shining from the giant idols in Pyongyang, the nation is a black hole. If there was a satellite image that could show the light of freedom and the lack of it on the peninsula, the contrast might be even greater.

During this time of darkness and silence in North Korean history, it is also important to see the way in which it looks like the very order of nature has been turned upside down in that country. Droughts, storms, floods, and every conceivable way in which nature can punish that area seems to be happening.

In the 1990s, North Korea experienced a large shortage of food and it could not have happened at a worse time. With the collapse of the Soviet Union, the Russians had stopped financing the regime in Pyongyang and cash was getting tight. Kim Il Sung had been preaching for decades about a country and culture that could stand on its own two feet and thrive independent of other nations. In the 1990s he had his chance to prove it...and failed miserably.

Since the removal of Russian funds, North Korea has had chronic famine. In the 1990s it can't be proven how many people died of hunger, but most conservative estimates are higher than 10% of the population.

On May 15, 2001, their own deputy foreign ministers reported at the UNICEF conference in Beijing that more than 220,000 people had died from famine between 1995 and 1998. Life expectancy fell from 73.2 in 1993 to 66.8 in 1999. The infant mortality rate went from 27 to 48 per 1,000 people. In 1994, 86 percent of the people had access to clean water and in 1996 just over half had access to clean water. The rate of polio and measles vaccinations fell from 90 percent to just 50 percent. These are the official numbers from the government, which was undoubtedly trying to paint a good picture! The situation on the ground was certainly much worse.

Most experts say that between 2 to 5 million people died during the 1990s in North Korea. The survivors must have wished they were dead at times, because they were being led by a madman who had no clue how to fix the country's problems. More than 80% of North Korea is mountainous, so when the farmers were forced to keep boosting the output of rice and maize, they soon exhausted all the nutrients in the soil.

Next, the leadership forced the people to level mountains by hand and begin growing crops on the more fertile land. All over North Korea, workers, not just farmers, could be seen terracing the mountains and cutting down trees to make way for new crops. None of these plans would be approved by anyone who knew a thing about farming. All of these disastrous ideas were coming from the leadership, which emphasized increased production at any cost. Any farmer who owned their own land and provided their own goods for sale on the market would never have made such foolish and careless decisions.

Kim had abused the environment long enough and it was about to get back at him. Soon after these plans were carried out, a rainy season came. With mountains loosened by terrace farming and no tree roots to hold the dirt in place, huge mudslides dumped into every valley and destroyed all the crops. The lack of crops led to a massive loss of livestock all over the country. Kim Il Sung then thought that the dead carcasses could contribute to organic fertilizer for the next harvest, but that was another complete disaster. South Korea also had floods and droughts, but they didn't suffer from a leader who rejected God and persecuted His followers.

Most of the people in North Korea today now rely on support from the U.S., Japan, and South Korea, but may never know about it. The Koreans are taught to praise Kim Il Sung and Kim Jong Il for everything that they receive. The very people responsible for the problems in North Korea are the ones that the people are forced to give thanks to.

Missionary doctors, dentists, and eye specialists go into North Korea to provide free medical care, but the leaders get the credit. Food from Christian nations is sent to areas devastated by famine; the leaders get the credit. The years of silence and darkness have been the modus operandi for years in North Korea, but that might soon be coming to an end.

6

THE WESTERN MISSION MODEL IN NORTH KOREA

H as the dominance of the Western model for missions ended? What has it meant for North Korea?

We have been exploring the history of missions in North Korea and established that Christianity in North Korea is unique because it was first brought there by Koreans themselves and initially promulgated without significant foreign influence. The major revivals however were fueled by the dedication of the more traditional Western missionaries. These missionaries brought many changes to the Korean peninsula and were indeed part of the traditional Western missionary model.

What is this model and how is it unique? What are its obvious strengths and weaknesses? How does the United States and Europe currently conduct missions in North Korea? Does it differ from the Biblical model? Is it conducive for church growth or a hindrance? Is it key to reaching North Koreans today?

In answering these questions, it is first necessary to look at the entire missionary enterprise in the West and see what kind of impact it is having. Have you ever been to a mission headquarters in America or Europe? Many—though not all—of them have Vatican-like status within their own denomination or social bubble. Housed in massive multi-million-dollar buildings, these organizations boast armies of secretaries and other staff who run around getting coffee and making travel arrangements for agency representatives and "missions experts" who look more like CEOs from Fortune 500 companies than any evangelist found in the pages of Scripture.

The Western missionary enterprise has thought up a great number of ways to spread the word about missions, using merchandise like books, t-shirts, wristbands, etc. The technology for reaching the lost is constantly developing as well, with various gadgets like MP4 players, solar-powered DVD players, and audio Bibles becoming common tools for evangelism in the field. There are more missionaries and full time mission staff employed today than ever before, but it seems that many of the groups have become more about the products than what those products were ultimately created for.

It seems like there is a new ministry popping up every other day, which is by no means a bad thing, but with all of the organizations, products, and electronic toys, shouldn't the Western mission model be producing far more fruit than it is? With all these advances, one would think that Western missions would be able to spread the gospel so quickly that Christ could return tomorrow and the whole world would know His name, yet that clearly isn't the case.

The Western mission model can be described in one word: centralized. Traditionally, it has always been very centralized around a structured chain of command complete with bureaucracy and strict guidelines for operation.

The Western mission model with this centralized command structure has been the dominant force on the field for several hundred years. Over the centuries they have rightly committed an inestimable amount of resources to the field. However, in recent years, they have tended to marginalize most Christians. Typically, Western mission agencies are organizations that have set up a system that relies heavily on giving. In order to make this giving more successful, mission agencies are run like assembly lines with designated workers for each stage of production. On the production line there are senders, organizers, promoters, and those that are sent—the missionaries themselves. This system has been effective in many ways, but it has also contributed to the Western churches slipping into a dangerous pattern of believing that their responsibility to the Great Commission is no more than their small part on the assembly line.

The Western mission model, for all its good points, has effectively marginalized large portions of society by making evangelical foreign missions the dominant expression of the Great Commission. Cross-cultural missionaries are our heroes and the exalted saints in our congregations. The rest of us tend to be viewed as "just senders." This has contributed to the evangelical church falling into a sad pattern over the last 50 years, creating large numbers of "pew warmers" who are all too happy to hear the heroic stories of missionaries without actually participating in the battle themselves. They may shed a tear and drop some change on a plate passing by, but the average churchgoer in the West rarely goes much beyond that when it comes to obeying the Great Commission.

Being centralized has helped in theological purity, but it has also contributed greatly to the bottleneck on the field. The "harvest is ripe, but the laborers are few" and mission agencies unfortunately help keep it that way. Mission agencies in the West, for the most part, do not have an endless supply of finances so they have a basic need to be careful who they send, where they send to, and what projects they participate in. However, this centralized leadership can easily become a dominant force in mechanically selecting projects and people without any direction from the Spirit of God.

Such a mechanical reliance on bureaucracy and policy has affected many projects in North Korea. In 2004-2005, workers with the Chinese missionaries had a vision to help use small MP3 players to get the gospel into North Korea. The initial idea was to provide an audio Bible with a well-known audio Bible device that was being used in other places around the world. With more research it was discovered that the most common audio Bible being used on the mission field was too big, didn't have enough storage capacity, and was too expensive. Obviously the distributors weren't competing in the real world. They were only selling the devices to Christian organizations that didn't have the ability or initiative to produce or purchase them elsewhere.

One of the main administrators of this project worked with a very small team to keep the project clandestine. A new audio device was located and utilized for the team of Chinese evangelists to use on the field. However, God began to speak clearly that there was one main person who should be included in this small group. This man represented a large international missions organization that is highly respected around the world. When he was introduced to the idea he pulled out a hand full of papers where God had been speaking to him about this very project. He had even been writing a gospel presentation to be put in audio format.

He began to get very excited about reaching the millions suffering in darkness in North Korea with this new method and he couldn't wait to share it with his mission board. He wrote up a proposal and introduced it to them, but to his surprise the mission board didn't want to have anything to do with the project. They frowned on the idea of being involved in an illegal activity like sending audio Bibles into North Korea.

The missionary was stunned and didn't know how to

react. He was certain he had heard from God, but he could not go against the authorities on the mission board. Eventually he shared with the board that he was certain God had given him this opportunity and was unable to discontinue his participation in the project. The board responded that if he did decide to continue they didn't want to know anything about it. If they became aware of his activities then they would be forced to take action. The mission board, to their credit, was willing to turn a blind eye to the situation for a while, but in the end it eventually led to the missionary resigning from the organization.

This same scenario has played out again and again throughout the history of missions. A well-known event took place in June of 1981 when a former U.S. Marine working in the Philippines felt the Lord tell him to deliver 1 million Bibles to China. This was an impossible task in those days, but Brother David was convinced that God was telling him to do it and he began stepping out in obedience. Along the way he was encouraged by Brother Andrew, another well-known Bible smuggler.

Brother David worked hard to make the operation, later known as "Project Pearl," a reality. He constructed a barge, and ran secret practice missions on the small islands in Hong Kong in preparation for delivery of Bibles to Guandong Province.

However, before he was able to purchase the tugboat needed for delivery, his organization and the leadership tried to shut down the operation. They gave him a clear directive to shut everything down. David was obligated to submit to the organization, but was also committed to what he felt the Lord had specifically told him to do. Instead of abiding by the organizational structure, David risked it all, bought a tugboat, and made the delivery helped by a major donation from Pastor Chuck Smith of Calvary Chapel Costa Mesa, California. In spite of the organization, Brother David was able to make his delivery that foggy night in June of 1981. Even thirty years later, "Project Pearl" Bibles are treasured in the hands of believers all over China.

Another example of this inherent problem in the Western mission method is Bible printing. When it comes to printing Bibles, there is a desperate need for Western organizations to better understand the investment side of the strategy. Their investments for God's Kingdom are good and help spread the gospel, but become a problem when the trend shifts away from the purpose of the investment and those in control resist change (even when the change is beneficial for evangelism). Then the investment becomes the central focus and not the mission. A missionary who has been involved in printing more than 11 million Bibles in China and distributing them out to the House Church reports his experiences between competing factions over Bible printing:

> I was meeting one of the largest names in Bible printing in the world. We met at Hong Kong International Airport. It was 2007 and the Beijing Olympics were less than a year away. He began to share with me about an opportunity he had to put Bibles in the drawer of every hotel room in Beijing. I was excited. I had been delivering Bibles in secret with my partners in China for years and to be able to openly place them in every hotel in Beijing seemed to be an absolute answer to prayer.
>
> I asked him how we could help. Anything we could do to be apart of this amazing opportunity would be great. However, he told me that the main thing they needed was funding to print the Bibles in another Asian country and arrange people to take them into China. I was shocked. I said, "We haven't printed Bibles outside of China for years. It is much easier and cheaper with much less risk

to print the Bibles inside China."

The man's voice dropped lower and his eyes were quite serious when he looked at me and said, "Yes, but printing them inside of China like you do is against the law and we don't want to break the law of China."

"And smuggling them into China in the luggage of foreigners is legal?" I quickly responded. The man just smiled, unable to answer my question. The meeting was over.

The large Bible printing agency had invested a lot of money and manpower into setting up a printer in another Asian country, so to use one inside of China would make his operation obsolete. He needed to justify carrying the Bibles, because it was the way they had always done it."

The system was already in place and the gears were already turning. The organizational leadership had already played their hand and made clear the direction that they wanted things to go in. Change was not an option, even if it meant attacking others who were doing things differently and more efficiently.

The first missionaries came to Korea to preach the gospel, but later on many missionaries came to teach their denominational theology and create their own fiefdoms. Because of the large size and multi-layered system of the Western mission model, it makes it more difficult (but not impossible) to hear from God, let alone be used by Him.

Centralized command is one of the main characteristics of Western-style missions because of the flow of funds. The command structure mirrors the image of this flow and the authority is reinforced by those funds. This centralized method contributes to the division of duties and categorization that places boxes around individuals and often prohibits (or at least discourages) any direct involvement in missions.

Either intentionally or unintentionally, many Western missionaries arrive on the mission field with a sense of superiority, a feeling that is reinforced by their living standards (which are often much higher than that of the locals). This superiority is also represented by the members of their missions board. Very few international mission boards have members that represent the countries they serve in. Western mission boards are much less likely to be involved in doing projects that don't require funding, because the power structure requires money to maintain authority and adherence to policy in the local environment.

Coincidentally, Western mission models tend to rely a lot more on fundraising and the consistent application of official policy and a lot less on the supernatural. Most of the agenda for the Western mission model is grounded very firmly in the Western business model.

An example in the Old Testament provides a useful illustration. In the book of Joshua, God tells Joshua to take the people of Israel and cross the Jordan into the Promised Land. Joshua did as God instructed and the people of Israel miraculously crossed through the Jordan as God split the waters in front of the Ark. Joshua obeyed and God worked a miracle.

If the same task was given to a Western missions board today, you would probably see a completely different scenario. Most likely, an exploration committee would be formed to go and see the river and assess the situation. A contracting company would then be asked to give an estimate for building a bridge and maybe even a bid war would begin between a couple of contracting committees. A budget would then be put together and submitted to the board. The budget would consist of flow charts, pie charts, timelines, deadlines, and page after page of technicalities all to be voted on by the board. Once a budget was set, marketers would start a fundraising campaign using flashy brochures, tear-jerking videos, speaking engagements, and massive online advertising on the most popular Christian websites.

After the fundraising, a reevaluation of the budget would be carried out and construction would begin. Permits would be changed, commissioners would need to be bribed, workers would be injured, lawsuits would be filed, late night phone calls would be made, and after a lot of sleepless nights, hard work, blood, sweat, and tears – the bridge over the river would be completed.

Completion would call for a ribbon-cutting ceremony— a photo-op for future fundraising that couldn't be missed— where everyone would pat each other on the back and praise God for something that was done completely without the need of Him getting in the way and messing things up with a miracle.

All this is not to say that God doesn't still use the Western church; indeed he uses it greatly. He still uses Western missionaries despite all their bureaucracy, smug behavior, and elitist ways, but His Spirit is moving greatly in the churches in the East and the winds are changing.

Saul went to war with the Philistines fully equipped with all the armor he had trained in and was comfortable using. During the days of King Saul, the armor, the sword, and the shield were effective. However, Saul's battle gear couldn't be forced on David in the battle to defeat the giant. All that heavy armor was not made for David. If David had gone out to fight Goliath with King Saul's gear he would have most certainly been killed. It is the same with world missions today.

Instead of trying to trudge around in Saul's cumbersome armor, David has a special calling and his battle strategy is going to be different. The battleground is different and the rules of the fight have changed, but he goes off to war with the power of the Lord's anointing. The church in the East is rising up to fight the giants of today, but there are mission agencies in the West determined to weigh David down with their own armor. They are trying to force the churches of Asia and Africa to wear the same battle garb they have been wearing for years, but just as the faithful steed of old is no match against tanks on the modern battlefield, Western mission models are too out-dated for fighting the enemies of the church in the East.

Indeed, a mighty battle cry is rising out of the East that has never been heard before. They have been silent for years, but the Spirit of the Lord is upon them and they can keep silent no longer. This rising army is the one God is using to do the most effective and lasting missionary work in North Korea.

As a Westerner that has observed over a decade of so-called "mission" work in North Korea, I, the co-author, was taken aback by the lack of results. Western mission organizations have poured literally millions of dollars into that country with pitifully little spiritual fruit. I have come to the reality that North Korea will most certainly be reached with the gospel, but not by Western missionaries. North Korea will be reached by the Chinese House Church.

Of the many Western missionaries working in the area, only one has testified to ever leading a North Korean to Christ. From the Chinese House Church we see entirely different results. Through the efforts of just 7 Chinese Back to Jerusalem missionaries, over 6,000 North Koreans have been brought to Christ in just a couple years. Why is this so?

It seems that the Western form of Christianity and missions seems weak to the Asian world. In a time when we need valiant warriors—true soldiers that will draw the sword and charge headlong into the ranks of the enemy without any thought of turning back—we Westerners exhibit a Christianity that is about retreats, tourist-like, short-term mission trips and entertainment.

Some of the greatest soldiers in history died for their country's cause. I have been in combat with men that would have laid down their life for me. As a matter of fact, that was their job, if need be, so that I could accomplish my mission.

John 15:13 says, *"Greater love has no one than this, that someone lay down his life for his friends."*

Those words of Christ explain why the Chinese are literally taking the gospel to the world while the West is entertaining itself to death. We aren't ready to die out of love for others, but the Chinese are.

The Apostle Paul mentioned in 2 Corinthians 5:8, *"Yes, we are of good courage, and we would rather be away from the body and at home with the Lord."* He knew he was saved, but wasn't yet ready to be offered. His next words were *"So whether we are at home or away, we make it our aim to please him."* This had nothing to do with his salvation; his motivation to stay in this world was to please Christ and be ready to face the judgment seat of Christ that all Christians will face (v.10).

In his letter to the Philippians he expresses his desire to go but the immediate need to stay for the sake of the church, *"I am hard pressed between the two. My desire is to depart and be with Christ, for that is far better. But to remain in the flesh is more necessary on your account."*(Philippians 1:23-24) Finally, we see in 2 Timothy 4:6-8 that he is ready to go:

> *For I am already being poured out as a drink offering, and the time of my departure has come. I have fought the good fight, I have finished the race, I have kept the faith. Henceforth there is laid up for me the crown of righteousness, which the Lord, the righteous judge, will award to me on that Day, and not only to me but also to all who have loved his appearing.*

We, as Christians, are not ready to die until we have fought a good fight of faith, finished our course, and kept the faith. Then, and only then, are we ready to receive our reward. Most aren't ready for reward because they don't want to even think about how little, if any, there would be. Most aren't ready to die. Paul was ready. The House Church in China is as well and that is why they are seeing such great fruit in North Korea.

The following is a quite infuriating example of a Chinese missionary's interaction with Western and South Korean missionaries. In this account it becomes painfully clear who are trying to save their lives (often acting as pure cowards) and who are willing to lose theirs for the sake of the gospel:

[While I was being held and interrogated in North Korea], my husband in China hadn't heard any news about me for a week, so he went to some missionaries and asked them to pray. **Of course there are missionaries with faith, but when something explodes there are many who think with human wisdom, saying, "Ah! Because this person was caught, we need to get away quickly."**

They said to my husband, "don't come to us anymore," changed their phone numbers, and disappeared. Missionaries are so sure that the person who was caught has already told everything to the police, but that's not always the case. It depends on the person. I've been caught in North Korea and China, but no missionary or anyone else's name or anything has ever come out because of me. Before God I can solemnly testify to this.

Just like in the Bible when Paul and Silas praised God in the prison cell and prayed for the people outside the prison, I also prayed in prison for the safety of the missionaries outside and for the Lord to guard my mind, heart and lips. However, whenever missionaries hear that someone is caught they think that 100% of the time the people are forced to take some drug (truth serum) and talk... NO! In my multiple imprisonments I was never once given that drug.

While I was gone the people who were supposed to help my family and pray with them on the contrary ran away from them and greatly hurt them. When I heard about it, it was even hard for me to bear. I worked only for God, not man. God knows!

I later was checked at the hospital and found out that from that big trauma I got a tumor in my body but couldn't afford surgery. After that time North Korean refugees kept seeking me out endlessly, so I fed and clothed them and taught them the Bible without any chance to rest. I thought I was going to die, but the God who saved me from the tiger's mouth knew about the tumor in my body, so I didn't tell anyone and just prayed. **There wasn't anyone to go to anyway because all the missionaries had changed their phone numbers and run away.**

It wasn't until nothing bad was happening to me that missionaries from all over came looking for me. At that time I met a missionary and missions team. I shared my testimony and while the team repented and prayed for me God told them that I needed to be admitted to a hospital, so they were willing to pay for everything and told me to have surgery right away. In that way, by God's grace through those people, I was able to get surgery.

At another time, when I met some Christians after being released from a Chinese prison, they hurt me by saying, "Americans and South Koreans can get out of jail easily, why did you get out like them?" implying that us poor Chinese are not as valuable as they are. Man decides who is valuable or not, but God is the same past, present, and future and doesn't care where you are born or grow up. People make a distinction between different colors of people, but God does not.

I've lived in China, North Korea, and South Korea. South Korea is supposed to be the Christian country among those three, but I was amazed to find out that the "Christian nation" is utterly rotten.

Nobody gets into this kind of work for the money, only because of God. So when [a famous mission organization] tried to offer me money for the publishing rights to my testimony, I was totally shocked and appalled. **They seemed more concerned with money than with the salvation of lost souls.**

With testimonies like this, it is no wonder that God seems to be turning elsewhere to bring His precious truth into North Korea. The seeker-friendly gospel of the West with it's emphasis on what God can do for you has created a church where very few—even among missionaries—are willing to first deny themselves and take of their cross before following Him.

Fig. 1. A torture stone used to strangle Korean Catholics during the violent persecutions of the 19th century

Fig. 2. Jeoldusan ("Beheading Mountain") is the cliff on which countless Catholics were beheaded during the great persecution of 1866. The bodies were thrown into the Han River below, which ran red with the blood of the martyrs. Today the Jeoldusan Martyr's Shrine sits atop the site.

Fig. 3. The headstone of missionary Homer Hulbert in Yanghwajin Foreign Missionary Cemetery shows the great love and dedication foreign missionaries had for the Korean people.

Fig. 4. The graves of Horace G. Underwood—the first Protestant missionary to enter and reside in Korea (1885)—and several family members. The Underwoods are famous for their medical work in Korea and the establishment of what would later become Yonsei University.

Fig. 5. An old postcard showing an aerial view of Pyongyang and Daedong River in the 1930s (*Archives*)

Fig. 6. A souvenir postcard from the 1930s showing street evangelism in Pyongyang. The gospel was an everyday part of the city's culture. (*Archives*)

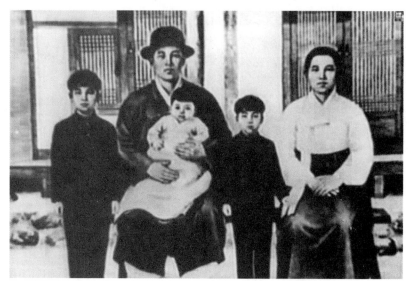

Fig. 7. 1 Kim Il Sung's family before leaving for Manchuria in 1920. From left to right: Kim Sung-Ju (a.k.a. Kim Il Sung); his father, Hyoung-jik; brothers Young-Ju and Chul-Ju (both killed by the Japanese); and his mother, Kang Banseok (whose name means "the Rock," referring to Christ). (*North Korean Archives*)

Fig. 8. Women take to the streets in the March First Movement of 1919.

Fig. 9. Executed members of the March First Movement. According to one eyewitness, the Japanese mockingly said, "*Since they are Christians, [executing them] in this way can get them to paradise*" and crucified them.

Fig. 10. Chinese Premier Wen Jiabao pays respect to Mao Anying, son of the late Chinese leader Mao Zedong, at a cemetery for Chinese soldiers in North Korea on October 5, 2009. (*Xinhua News/Huang Jingwen*)

Fig. 11. A prison in China near the North Korean border that holds North Korean refugees before sending them back to the North. There have been numerous reports of suicides here by those who would simply rather die than be repatriated and tortured to death.

Fig. 12 & 13. Previously unreleased images taken with a hidden camera of Chinese soldiers executing North Korean refugees. Their only crime: fleeing their country to find food.

Fig. 14. The body of a North Korean floats in the Tumen River. For decades North Koreans have been fleeing to China across this river, but many never make it across.

Fig. 15. A bridge into North Korea over the Tumen River. Although this river has meant death for many, it has also become a source of life as food, clothing, medicine, and the gospel are frequently carried across it by evangelists.

Fig. 16. The Juche Tower in Pyongyang has a torch on top that represents the Spirit of the People. (*38north.org*)

Fig. 17. A North Korean calendar showing the year 2011 as "Juche 100."

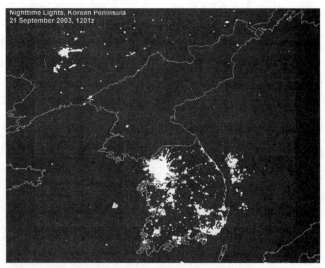

Fig. 18. The Korean Peninsula seen from space at night (*Defense Meteorological Satellite Program*)

Fig. 19. Portaits of Kim Il Sung and Kim Jong Il on an office wall.

Fig. 20. A typical monument found in every North Korean town square that states, "The Great Leader Comrade Kim Il Sung is forever with us."

Fig. 21. Anti-American propaganda: "When under duress, [victory] through a heavy blow. When chastised, [victory] through merciless punishment."

Fig. 22. Anti-American propaganda: "American Imperialists, don't recklessly rampage!"

Fig. 23. Looking across the border into North Korea at the Joint Security Area of Panmunjom, Demilitarized Zone (DMZ)

Fig. 24. A North Korean praise song called "The Song of General Kim Il Sung"

Fig. 25. Back to Jerusalem missionaries in training to go to North Korea meet for prayer

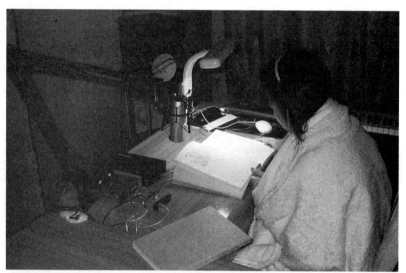

Fig. 26. Back to Jerusalem missionaries record an audio Bible in a North Korean dialect at a makeshift underground recording studio. Thousands of North Koreans have come to Christ by listening to this audio Bible on MP3 players sent into their country.

Fig. 27. Boxes of MP3 players before assembly for distribution in North Korea

Fig. 28. North Koreans are required to wear these Kim Il Sung lapel pins as a sign of devotion to their government and their undying love for the "Great Leader." Here is but a small sampling of those given by new North Korean Christians to Back to Jerusalem missionaries as a sign of their commitment to follow Christ and shun idolatry, no matter what the cost.

7

A NEW GENERATION

I t was October of 2009 and Mrs. Pak (not her real name) sat in the private room of a coffee shop in China, a literal stone's throw away from North Korea. Although she is about fifty years old, her face still shows the joy of a young girl. Mrs. Pak is one of the very few people in the world who has been in both Chinese and North Korean prisons and is willing to talk about it. She represents a growing number of Chinese who are taking the gospel of Jesus Christ into North Korea. While the world is waiting for the South to cross the 38th Parallel with a warm and fuzzy, health and wealth, seeker-friendly gospel or Western missionaries to gallantly gallop in on white horses and save the day, the Chinese are already going into North Korea and boldly proclaiming the gospel.

Mrs. Pak comes from a long line of Christians in her family that goes all the way back to the revivals of Jonathan Goforth. As she lowers her eyes contemplatively and pulls her hair back behind her ear she recalls the day that God called her to preach to the North Koreans:

"I heard the voice of the Lord call out to me," she said. "The Lord called out to me, 'Feed my sheep. Feed my sheep. Feed my sheep.'"

"But I told Him, 'Sorry Lord, I am not capable. I am not educated enough. I am not strong enough. I am not good enough. I don't know how to preach. I am a nobody. I feel that I would be a good worker, use me for labor. I am not smart and I don't know the Bible very well. I want to feed your sheep in North Korea, but I am not able to preach.'"

Little did she know that God would use her mightily to preach His message throughout North Korea. Mrs. Pak was a Chinese national of Korean origin. Her native language is Korean, but she speaks enough Chinese to get by in her day-to-day tasks as an insurance saleswoman.

The eager American that was sharing coffee with her began to ask Mrs. Pak about her experiences in North Korea. The following is from that interview:

Mrs. Pak: *I was born here in China to a Korean family. Though I am Chinese, I don't really feel like I belong in China because I can't really speak the language well and my culture is totally different. However, when I am in Korea, I don't feel Korean either because my culture has been somewhat changed from living in China my entire life. So I can't really say that I have an identity to a single country. However, my burden is clear – it is for the people in North Korea who really need Jesus.*

I am married, but my husband left in July 2009 to work at a golf course in South Korea to bring in extra money for our family. Our son will be going to college soon and we will need the extra money for him. I have one son and he is 15 years old. My husband and I are not sure how long he will be living there. I feel like I am a mother to many of the people inside of North Korea. I spent several years working inside North Korea, preaching the gospel of Jesus Christ. However, since I was arrested and put in jail I have been working and helping as best I can on this side [China side] of the river.

Interviewer: Were you arrested inside North Korea or in China?

Mrs. Pak: *Both.*

Interviewer: Both? Do you feel comfortable telling me about that?

Mrs. Pak: *Before I was able to go into North Korea, I needed a visa. I didn't know how to get one. I prayed and prayed and then one day God answered my prayer. I have a friend whose brother owned a trading company that worked inside North Korea. I shared with my friend about my burden to preach there and my friend felt moved in her spirit to help me get a visa through her brother. The brother gave me a North Korean visa without any questions. I didn't even have a position in the company. I didn't know anything about their business. I just had a visa and went inside.*

Interviewer: Did the North Korean officials say anything about that?

Mrs. Pak: *Oh yes, they looked at my visa paperwork and told me that I would have to pay them a bribe if I wanted to go through, but my response was, "I am sorry, but I don't have anything to pay you with. If you want money* *you will have to get it from my boss because he hasn't given me any." They would always look at me as if I were not worth their time and pass me through as quickly as possible. Once they knew that I was too poor to pay them anything, they never attempted to get money from me again as a bribe.*

Once inside, I had many opportunities to preach the gospel. Oh yes, I never went where I was supposed to – I mean, I didn't even have a job, so there was no reason to go to the main office. I went to villages along the road from the bridge at the border to a major coastal city and met with people in villages and shared the gospel.

Interviewer: Did anyone ever listen to you? Did you ever see anyone come to Christ?

Pak: *Certainly! There were several people who wanted to turn me in to the police, but those people thought that I might be of more value to them if I were able to continue coming to their village. They saw me as a person who could provide things from outside the country for them. However, I met with Christians and shared the gospel message with them and also was able to share with others who were not Christians—seeing some of them come to Christ. The Bible was really very rare. Those that had a Bible only had portions of it. They would have parts of it buried under their wooden floors or hidden in the walls and they would take it out and read it in pieces. This small part of God's Word was able to sustain the faith of several believers who are inside of North Korea. I regularly met with many different Christians inside, more than 100 believers. Unfortunately I was not able to bring them Bibles* because I didn't take in things like that, but I did take in lots of food and rice. I would get a truck and fill it with 1 or 2 tons of rice and drive to North Korea and wait until evening, then I would drive to villages and people would surround the truck and I would hand out rice.

Interviewer: Is that even possible? We have delivered many tons of rice and we were never able to go to villages and deliver it to any place we wanted to. The government keeps a strict policy on these types of humanitarian projects.

Pak: *Oh, but the guards knew me. They knew who I was. Even though I didn't give them money, I did bring them things and help them. I helped them and they helped me. The immigration officials and border guards became my friends and I was able to do many things like this. Even when I was arrested, I think that my friendship with them helped me a lot.*

Interviewer: Can you tell me more about your time in prison?

Pak: *Yes, in 2005, I was traveling inside North Korea, preaching the Gospel, when a person in one of the villages turned me in. The police came to where I was staying, busted into the room, and told me that I was an enemy of the state. I was taken into an interrogation room and questioned day and night. I wasn't given water or food for days. The commander kept pounding on the desk in front of me, demanding to know every detail about what I have been doing and the names of the people I had been meeting with. I just kept telling him that I am a child* *of Christ and love the people of my homeland. There is nothing that I would do to harm anyone in my homeland. I was kept in prison for over a month, but because I was a Chinese citizen they let me go and sent me back to China. During my time in North Korea I made many contacts and many people grew to trust me, knowing that I loved them with the love of our Heavenly Father. So even when I didn't return to North Korea, the people still knew about me. Even today, I am called on a weekly basis to provide support for people when they come out of North Korea into China for supplies. I help all that I can. I get calls from many people who don't know who I am, but have heard about me and ask if I can help them.*

One night in 2007, I received a call from a man who said that he was a Christian friend of mine from North Korea and had just come across the border illegally and needed my help. I asked him to meet up with me so I could provide him some support. When I arrived at the meeting place, the man that came to meet with me asked many, many strange questions and didn't seem eager to move to any other location, which I found to be odd. I didn't know that the man was an undercover member of the PSB [Chinese police]. I was arrested and interrogated. The special police unit wanted to know everything about my "operations." I was put in prison and was given a life sentence. As I sat in prison I did the only thing that I knew to do and that was to pray. However, in the prison there was a woman who did not like me because she knew that I was a Christian. She hated Christians. She was a fellow inmate and the guards relied upon her to provide information to them about the other inmates. This helped them tremendously in keeping order in the prison.

Whenever I prayed, she would yell across the prison block and tell the guards that I was praying. The prison guards would come and hit me and shout at me to stop praying. I could see the delight in the woman's eyes when the guards hit me. She enjoyed seeing me punished because of her hatred of Christians. Her anger and hatred was intense. Even though they beat me, I was not able to stop praying. I didn't know what else to do. It was the only thing that I knew could really help me. The guards realized that they could not make me stop, so they made me get on my knees, put my hands on my legs, keep my back straight, and look straight ahead. I was not allowed to close my eyes. Whenever I bowed my head, the woman would shout out to the guards and they would come running and punish me. I didn't know what else to do so I began to fast. The woman then yelled to the guards and said that I wasn't eating because I was praying even more. They punished me even more. However, over time, the woman started sitting next to me and we would talk. I shared with her about the never-ending love of Jesus and how He loves us no matter what we have done and can be with us no matter where we are. One day she received Jesus Christ as her Lord and Savior. She would pray and sing with me and even prayed and sang when I wasn't around. The prison guards left her alone. They didn't want to punish her or make her hate them because she was such a valued asset. She kept the prison under control so if they lost her as an ally, things could get very ugly in the prison very fast. The prison didn't want to see me stay much longer, so they made me an offer: if I paid money, I would be set free. They called my family and my family tried to come up with the money, but it was very difficult. God showed me in a dream that I would be released from prison soon.

At that very moment there were churches in South Korea that had heard about my situation and began to pray for me and donated part of the money needed to get me out of prison.

My family came and paid the money and I was released. My husband begged me to never again preach the gospel. He felt that it was too dangerous for me. For a short time, I listened to him, but I truly feel that my life is not my own. My life does not belong to me. It belongs to God and He is the one who leads me and guides me. Against his wishes and the wishes of my family I continued to preach the gospel of Jesus Christ to anyone who will lend a ear, but my main focus is for the people of North Korea. That is where my burden is.

Mrs. Pak represents the new generation of Korean-Chinese who are ready to take the gospel into North Korea. These Chinese citizens get more opportunities than any other group of people. Many of them have family members who live inside North Korea and oftentimes, annually, they would receive permission to go and visit their families. They have the opportunity to go and see how their families are doing, take them supplies, food, money, and—most important of all—they are able to share the gospel.

Mrs. Pak became well known among the North Korean refugee community. Many North Korean refugees began to share her phone number with others, knowing that she would help them if they needed it. She provided food, money, clothing, and even training to North Koreans who were new Christians. She would train them in the foundational truths of Christianity and send them back into North Korea.

Mrs. Pak was the woman who could help anyone at any

time, but there were times when she was the one that needed help. October 2009 was one of those times. She needed help that she could not get from anywhere else. She called her American friend who used to be in the military and would smuggle drugs into the U.S. from Mexico before he came to the Lord. He was used to conducting operations in secrecy, but this time he was being asked to do it for the Lord.

Pak was helping a North Korean brother who was a new Christian named Mr. Lee (not his real name). Mr. Lee was fresh out of prison. He had been imprisoned for three years when the locals heard a rumor of him becoming a Christian. When he was finally released, Mr. Lee went home and found his family starving, with no food and no warm clothing. They had no real way to survive the coming winter. Mr. Lee's family pleaded with him to take a chance and try to go to China to find food, money, and warm clothing to bring back to North Korea. It was the only chance that the family had to make it through North Korea's harsh winters. The family reasoned that Mr. Lee had already spent time in prison and had the least to lose if he got caught at the Chinese border.

The border of China and North Korea is marked by the Amnok (Yalu) and Tumen Rivers. The entire border is guarded by both Chinese and North Korean troops, who will shoot trespassers on site. Illegal crossing is not tolerated under any circumstances.

Mr. Lee and his family were desperate. He risked his life to cross into a country that he didn't know anything about. When he arrived in China, he was told about Pak and he called her and asked for help. On the other side of the line was a sweet voice that was caring and loving. There was something different about Pak. She was not like the women in North Korea.

Mrs. Pak arranged for a driver to pick up Mr. Lee and bring him to the underground church. When he arrived he was given a warm and loving welcome from Pak. She provided him with a nice hot Korean meal and some new clothes. The members of the underground house church were also there to help Mr. Lee. Soon, Mr. Lee was surrounded by fellow Christians who cared about him. Mr. Lee stayed at the house for a few days and received intense theological training and prayer.

Pak's husband was working in South Korea, so Pak gave all of her husband's clothes to Mr. Lee, seeing that her husband had no immediate need for them. Pak was able to provide Mr. Lee with the money that he needed, along with blankets, electronic audio Bibles, and video players with *The Jesus Film* in the North Korean dialect.

There is always one major problem with every North Korean who illegally crosses the border into China to get supplies: getting back into North Korea. Both Pak and Lee were faced with the challenge of how to get back into North Korea. Pak called her American friend who had a car and could drive them to the river.

During that time, the American had two friends with him in town. They were both former military special operates. When darkness fell, all three of these men went to meet with Mr. Lee. When they arrived at the flat where Mr. Lee was staying, he was having a warm meal and eating as much as he could before leaving. Pak gave him a mobile phone that he could use to call from inside. It was a Chinese mobile phone that could get a signal whenever he was close enough to the border.

When the Americans came into the room, Mr. Lee was visibly nervous. He had never seen foreigners before. Little did he realize that he too was a foreigner. He ate his food with his face looking at the ground. The Americans shared with Pak their plan. They used small objects from the dinner table to represent the two vehicles they would use. The lead car would have the two Americans and the back car would have Mr. Lee.

If the authorities pursued them, the lead car would ram the police, distracting them so Mr. Lee's vehicle could escape and take him to a safe place. When the plan was laid out and a translation was given to him, Mr. Lee stopped eating and looked up. His eyes were as big as bowling balls as he asked in amazement, "You would do that for me?"

The Americans reassured him that they were his brothers, not his enemy. "We are all one. We are all brothers and sisters in Christ. We are part of the same family. Of course we would risk our lives for you." This message of dedication said more than any words could communicate between men from countries which have been mortal enemies for decades.

Mr. Lee had audio Bibles with him and intended to use them to evangelize in his village. "I have about 20 Christians in my village," he said with a stern smirk as he carefully placed the audio Bibles into his bag. The former military guys felt like they had stepped back in time and were back on the field, running operations. They were wearing all black, had laid out their plans, and were feeling nostalgic—until Mr. Lee pulled out his floatation device. To get back into North Korea, he would need to use a floatation device so his precious goods would not get wet. This device turned out to be a child's swimming ring, made out of pink plastic with purple elephants to boot! These combat veterans had never worked with such non-tactical gear before.

Both teams loaded into the vehicles. They drove down the dark roads along the river until they found a dark place by the railroad tracks. The team was driving at night with no lights along the road. Mr. Lee jumped out and disappeared into the night. He stripped down and put all of his clothes into an airtight bag, then placed the bag on his non-tactical floatation device. He quietly swam across the frigid river, pulling his bags across on the floating rings. Once he reached the other side, he put his clothes back on and crawled into the high weeds. He got as far as he could before daylight came and then kept himself hidden until nightfall, when he could carefully make his way home.

That was not Lee's last time going to China. He had found a route in and out of the country and had a group of friends there that were able to supply him and his family with things that they desperately needed. It was just the beginning of Lee's ministry to bring the light of the gospel into utter darkness. Though he met with a great deal of difficulties, of which will be told in a later chapter, the Lord used him in a mighty way. Indeed a new generation of Christian warriors has arisen in China and North Korea. They are not afraid to bear the cross— even unto death.

8

HERE COME THE REDS, HERE COMES THE CROSS

N orth Korea has a real problem on its hands. There was an invasion from the North in the 1950s and more than 60 years later there is another invasion taking place, but this one is from even farther north. Their northern Chinese brethren are experiencing the world's largest revival and they have no desire to enact a containment policy. In the 1940s and 50's the northern part of the Korean peninsula and bordering China were painted red with the sweeping reforms of communism, but today the map is turning red with the blood of Jesus covering the sins of those being caught up in the fires of revival.

The underground house church movement of China is completely unique in the world today, but is not unique in the history of the church. The church in China might have as many as 150 million believers and there are claims that more than 30,000 believers come to Christ daily. Of course these numbers are debatable, but even if they are only half that amount, it is still the world's largest revival.

Never before have so many people been transformed by the power of the gospel of Jesus Christ in so short a time as they are in China today. Communism did not just ruin the lives of millions of Koreans, but the Chinese as well. More than 70 million people died under the reign of Mao Zedong, but out of the ashes of Chinese communism and the cult following of Mao Zedong came a Christianity that is radical and on fire. Communism in China, Like Kim Il Sung in North Korea, attempted to place production and financial achievement above all else, but inside of man is the innate desire to serve the Creator. To have a relationship with the God of all creation is programmed into our DNA and nothing else will satisfy.

Religion is the most universal characteristic of all cultures, no matter how remote they may be and no matter how far back in time we look. When atheism and productivity alone did not meet the basic fundamental needs for man to pray to a higher God, the cult practice of praying to the leader was implemented. Like in North Korea, Mao was worshiped in China. His picture was placed on everyone's suit lapel and all homes were required to have a picture of Mao Zedong prominently displayed.

Benjamin, a famous Chinese singer who won a televised singing competition in China when he and his family sang a Christian song, remembers those days:

> I can remember when a member of our family was cleaning the picture of Mao. He wanted to honor the picture of Mao by keeping it perfectly clean even though the rest of his home was dirty and poor. He didn't have any proper cleaning detergent, so he heated up water and used that water to clean his portrait of Mao. However, the water and his rag were so hot that the steam ruined the paint of Mao's cheek. The paint came right off of the portrait! The man panicked. He did not have the money to buy a new one and could not afford to have the town see what he had done. It was a horrible mistake. Other relatives quickly came and publicly condemned him. Destroying a

picture of Mao Zedong was a punishable offense."

Many Chinese were convinced that they would have better lives if they could make money and become wealthier. Today, Chinese are wealthier than they have been in recent memory, but nothing that the economy can provide can replace the void that they have in their lives. Going overseas to find better education, purchasing the best car that money can buy, finding a high paying job, having plastic surgery in Thailand to look better, finding the perfect house, all of these things are but vanities of vanities. Many Chinese are finding their needs fulfilled at the cross of Jesus Christ.

In China, the people who are coming to Christ are not Sunday morning Christians and weekday infidels. They are radical, sold out, dedicated, and passionate believers. These Christians have been freed from slavery and are committed to glorifying the God who freed them. They are taking His message throughout China. Unfortunately for Kim Jong Il, they are not stopping at the borders of China. They are focused on reaching the rest of the world with the gospel of Jesus Christ.

These vast millions understand the darkness and hopelessness from which they came and desperately desire to pull others out of the same pit before it is too late. No one can relate more to the church in North Korea than the Chinese. The millions of souls coming to faith in Jesus throughout China did not come without a price. Hundreds of missionaries from faraway lands poured out their blood on Chinese soil so the seed of the gospel could grow. Any chance of reaching the church in North Korea is going to take the same sacrifice, dedication, and bloodshed that China did.

The parallel between the Chinese church and the North Korean church is truly amazing. For decades, Chinese Christians have endured all manner of suffering and deprivation for the sake of their Lord Jesus. Throughout the second half of the 20th century, countless numbers of Chinese believers were brutally beaten, tortured, imprisoned, and even killed for their faith. By the 1970s, it was believed that no Christians remained alive in China, but this was far from the truth. Today, many people also believe that there are few, if any, believers in North Korea. To many the thought of a vibrant church in North Korea sounds preposterous. Jesus said that a grain of wheat must fall into the ground and die before it can bear any fruit (John 12:24). The history of the Chinese church proves this truth and in due time we shall see it to be true of the church in North Korea as well.

Just when the rest of the world thought there weren't any Christians left in China, a revival started. People in China were desperate to get Bibles. The few Bibles still left in China were painstakingly copied by hand and distributed to various places. They were memorized, hidden, torn into smaller sections and separately buried for later retrieval. We hear of many similar things going on in North Korea today.

By the grace of God, the church in China grew into the massive body that it is today, which is not good news for the North Korean government. Unfortunately for their regime, the Chinese Christians actually have a vision for the peninsula. It is called the "Back to Jerusalem" vision.

It is important to understand the Back to Jerusalem vision because it is the vision of a massive movement in China that will undoubtedly impact the future of North Korea. There are a number of missionaries today from the Chinese underground house churches that are on the border of North Korea and are moving in and out of the country, both legally and illegally, proclaiming the gospel of Jesus Christ.

Along the China-North Korea border there are churches, Bible schools, mission schools, language schools, the refugee underground railroad, orphanages, safe houses, and whatever else the Christian can do to help the people in North Korea. An increasing number of these ministries are being established by the Chinese house churches.

Like the rival that has been going on in China, the Back to Jerusalem vision of the Chinese underground house church is also unique in the world today, but is not unlike the early history of the church. This vision can be found throughout the pages of Scripture and in the book of Acts. The term "Back to Jerusalem" as it is taught in the underground Chinese house churches can be summarized as the Great Commission for the Chinese church.

Jesus gave the Great Commission in Matthew 28:18-19 and Acts 1:8. The Great Commission is the command from Jesus to take the Good News to every tribe and tongue. This Great Commission has not been completed. There is an entire area from the border of China to the border of Israel that has not heard the gospel. This area is commonly referred to as the 10/40 Window. This term—contrary to many claims out there today—is a term that was coined by Luis Bush in 1990. He was referring to the regions of the eastern hemisphere located between 10 and 40 degrees north of the equator. This geographical location has the highest level of socioeconomic poverty of any place on earth and has the highest percentage of the least evangelized. Two-thirds of the world's population lives in this window and is predominately Muslim, Hindu, Buddhist, and Atheist (and Juche, of course). This area is not only the poorest area in the world, but is also the most hostile towards Christianity. It is also the focus of the least amount of mission resources. The 10/40 Window is the last frontier of the gospel. This is the last area of the world where the gospel has not penetrated in the traditional sense. This area between China and Jerusalem is also one of the areas of the world lacking the most basic human rights. North Korea fits right into this vision and the Chinese are focusing on getting the gospel into that country.

The Chinese are not like the Western missionaries. They are not as divided by competing theological differences, but instead have been refined by the fires of persecution. The church in China was free from the restrictions of Western thought and cynicism. Most of them did not know enough about Western "reason" to disbelieve what was written in the Bible. They had not been trained how to explain away the miracles of Jesus and the disciples. They didn't know better than to believe what God said in His word and as a result, the Chinese church is a great testimony to what God will do when people just take Him at His word.

When one American missionary was first approached about working with the Chinese, he was intrigued by the prospects, but after working with the first Chinese Back to Jerusalem missionaries, he has been completely sold out to serve the Chinese and their efforts to reach North Korea. This man had been called to bring the gospel to North Korea and is now working together with the Chinese and the Back to Jerusalem vision. During the fall of 2010, he was asked to introduce North Korea during a Back to Jerusalem meeting with Brother Yun, also known as the Heavenly Man:

"You know, I used to introduce myself as a missionary to North Korea, but today I would be happy to call myself a janitor working in the broom closet in the Chinese underground house church," he said as he stood before the crowd in Northern San Diego County.

The Back to Jerusalem missionaries have been working on getting the Bible into North Korea. One of the things that they are doing is getting small MP3 players into North Korea. The players are the size of a US quarter. The players have an introduction to the gospel, the Bible, testimonies from North

Koreans who have given their lives to Christ, and Christian worship music in their own musical style.

These MP3 players have been very effective in bringing the gospel of Jesus Christ to North Korea. Many letters and testimonies have come out of North Korea regarding the effectiveness of the audio Bible in the country.

From the labors of the Back to Jerusalem missionaries from China and by the grace of God, fruit is being produced in North Korea. The following are testimonies of North Koreans who have been reached through the Chinese House Church's missionary efforts:

A Letter of Gratitude from Mrs. "H"

I was very cold and scared when I escaped across the Tumen River. I was living day to day in Chosun [North Korea] and it was very hard and difficult. I was tired of this everyday. When the Grandmother that lived in China was coming back and forth and giving us help, life was bearable, but when that stopped, it became difficult, even to the point that I contemplated committing suicide. I had nothing.

When I got to the Grandmother's house in China safely, she told me God must have helped, and that Jesus is our Savior. Whenever she came to Chosun in the past, she gathered us together and told us that we had to believe in Jesus in order to have life, and pray to Him for relief from the famine. At first, it was hard to believe and I had a lot of questions, but through the [MP3] player we have realized the true love of Christians and of Jesus Christ, and from the man that brought us the player.

The current situation helped me realize that I have to trust Jesus Christ as my Savior. My mother and father had me 36 years ago and have raised me, but because of poverty their focus was to feed us, but never once embraced us. But, the people that gave us the player had never seen me before and did not share blood as family members yet they prayed in tears and embraced us and also gave us living expenses of 1,000 RMB.

This is the first time in my life I have ever received this kind of love. Indeed I felt the true human love. When it was explained to me through the player how God created the world and He has concern for everything I slowly understood who God and Jesus are. I came to know that in this world, only the Love of Jesus Christ can save a person, and a person must believe in Him to be saved. From now on, in Chosun, I will tell my family, my mother, my dear daughter, and my brother and sisters, I will tell them about Jesus and that He is our Savior, and He is the solution to our poverty. On top of that, if we want our country to be a community where there is no evil and lies, we must allow Jesus to cleanse our hearts and teach us to love others. He is the hope for our nation. I send the warmest gratitude and respect for those that are helping me and our people in Chosun.

I will tell my people in my hometown to believe in Jesus. I will pray God will use these words to help us to live more like real humans and to open our eyes to the truth. At last, I wish for your health that you will have the Spirit of Jesus and I thank those people who loved us and accepted us. Bye. –Mrs. H

(NOTE: This lady also took off her Kim Il Sung lapel pin and gave it to us as a sign she no longer wanted to be associated with the idolatry of leader worship and Juche in North Korea.)

The Testimony of Mr. "P"

We thank you for sending the players to us. When I first met _____ in _____, it was hard for me to believe. I knew of Jesus, but didn't believe. After hearing with my own ears on the player the story of God's love for us to allow Jesus to die, and be brought again to life, I believed the story and believed Jesus Christ is my Savior. Now, I am able to take the players into my country [North Korea]. Several people have believed in Jesus after receiving the players and we can now secretly be a family for God. I have shared with my son, daughter-in-law, wife, and neighbor by using the MP3 player. They are believers and meet with us now. Thank you to those who have helped.

The Testimony of Jin Sook

I am Jin Sook of _____, Chosun. I have been truly blessed to receive an MP3 from Ms. _____. She was able to receive some from people and give to our town. I heard the truth and became a believer. I am listening to the truth every day now and am being blessed. I will share my MP3 with others so they can see God is the true God that gave us Jesus to rescue us from sin. We can survive in hardship now because we can know we will be in paradise if anything should happen to us. For this reason I will share the truth and not worry. Mrs._____ is a good example for us because she has been able to share the gospel with many people, even though she is old and cannot see. Thank you so much. Pray I can share the truth with others just like it was given to me.

A Testimony from a Back to Jerusalem Missionary

It had been raining so badly inside North Korea that we could not get any work done. I told one of the workers I would pray for it to stop raining. It stopped. She asked me if my God really listened when I prayed. I told her, "of course." She wanted me to teach her how to pray. I told her I had to first teach her about God.

Later, she told another worker whose father had died that she should pray with me. After that, I talked with the girl that had first asked me about prayer. Tears streamed down her face and she called out to the Lord to save her. She is now a true believer in North Korea! I will use the projector to show her *The Jesus Film* so she can learn more about Jesus. Later, I will take a Bible on MP3 inside to her.

Mr. Kim Speaks

I was given an MP3 player inside Chosun. It had on it stories of how Chosun people had heard the Bible and were now believers in Jesus. I listened to the player. It also had the Bible, but I didn't believe. A month passed. I illegally went to China to get food, and some goods to try to sell. While I was there, I met people that tried to help me. They told me they were Christians. I knew what I had been listening to on the player was true, and I believed in Jesus. I am now taking some MP3 players inside, along with food that has been provided by Christians to me. I will give the food to people. When they ask why I am willing to help, I will tell them I am now a Christian, and will give them a player so they can become a Christian as well.

The Testimony of Mr. Cha

I became a Christian due to the fact that a lady I met

while sneaking into China gave me an MP3 player. I am now operating a small business, coming out of Chosun, getting products, and taking them back into Chosun to sell. The guards let me cross as long as I give them a percentage of my goods. I am not able to take MP3 players with me every trip, but about every third time I come to China, I return with some MP3 players to give people, along with some food. When people are being fed, they do not turn you in for being a Christian. Chosun people do not give food away, so they know I am different for helping and are willing to find out why. This makes giving them a player easy.

The Testimony of Mr. Jin

I am a Chinese Korean Christian. I have been able to place MP3 players in many shelters. The shelter operators then give them to North Koreans when they come out as refugees in China. Some of these refugees attempt to escape and go to South Korea. Others go back to North Korea. All of them take the MP3 Players with them. Even sometimes those that are caught trying to escape China to South Korea and are taken back to North Korea have been reported to witness to people in jail, truly believing till their death.

Not only have the MP3 players been effective, but Back to Jerusalem missionaries to North Korea have also been using very cutting edge electronics. In 2008, there were new models invented by 3M that had the potential to change much on the mission field; they invented a pocket-size projector. Back to Jerusalem missionaries began to use that unit on the field. The pocket-size projector was used to show *The Jesus Film* and other videos about the life of a Christian. Sermons were also placed on the projector so that new pastors can use them to minister sermons from pre-designated slides that are prepared for them.

The unit that is used today is the size of a smart phone, doesn't need a player, has built-in speakers, 2GB memory, an SD memory card chip, 5 hours of battery power, and is made of stainless steel. The leaders of the church can use the pocket-projector to show Christian videos and teachings for crowds of up to 20 people.

From the success in North Korea, churches around the world are starting to use it as well. From the Philippines to Iran and Morocco, the unit is proving to be very effective.

The beautiful thing about the Back to Jerusalem vision is that it is a vision that isn't owned by any denomination, group, or organization. No one owns the vision. No one claims exclusive rights to the vision of the Chinese church. Churches and networks in China disagree on many different things and sometimes are not even able to work together, but they all have the same basic Back to Jerusalem vision. No one can claim rights or control of the vision. It does not have a headquarters. It doesn't have a big shiny building on a hill overlooking the valley with hundreds of full-time staff shuffling through papers and emails. It doesn't have a monthly overhead of money going out for administration. Nor does it have a methodical system subject to a board, committee, or outside entity deciding what missionaries can or cannot be sent or what countries should or shouldn't be included.

The Chinese have been working together with the North Koreans for generations. China is really the only country in the world that is willing to work together with North Korea and the Chinese enjoy the most freedom in North Korea because of the official political relationship between the two countries. Chinese can be seen running restaurants, hotels, transportation services, and other major businesses throughout the special economic zones of North Korea.

The Chinese are welcomed as fellow communists and are not stereotypically Christian, so they are not as closely monitored as a Westerner would be. Chinese Back to Jerusalem missionaries also don't need large amounts of money to live. They are investing in platforms that will provide visas and living expenses as well as an avenue for sharing the gospel without the need for constant church donations. Today, many Chinese evangelists are living on less than $100 USD per month. That is much lower than the typical monthly budget of any Western missionary!

Despite the great amount of fruit God is producing in North Korea through the Back to Jerusalem missionaries, it is not an easy task. The devil won't go down without a fight and is pulling out all the stops to prevent North Korea from coming to Christ—even if it means using the Name Above All Names to trick people. There have been reports that the North Korean government is taking new steps to stop the clandestine spread of Christianity, particularly in the areas near the border of China. Such measures include infiltrating underground churches and setting up fake prayer meetings as traps for Christian converts. Unsuspecting Western and South Korean missionaries are often taken in by these ruses.

A foreign missionary working near one of North Korea's borders was excited to find a North Korean "refugee" looking for help in the city. She approached this missionary and asked him about God. The missionary got even more excited. She told him of hearing about God in North Korea, and how she knew that her government was wrong and that Bill Clinton was a true hero.

The missionary shared the gospel with this lady, who repeated a prayer after him. She stayed in China instead of going back to North Korea and was trained by the missionary for several weeks. She got to know his friends and co-laborers. Does this sound too good to be true? It was. Unfortunately, warnings giving by Chinese Christians suspicious of this woman went unheeded.

Suddenly things began to take a turn for the worse. In one fatal evening, an entire operation helping North Koreans both in North Korea and China was destroyed. Coworkers from North Korea were mysteriously arrested. Two were even shot by North Korean security patrols.

Chinese Christians with very fruitful ministries in North Korea were arrested or forced to flee at a moment's notice. Several foreign missionaries had to flee the country. One long-term missionary in China had to hide for two days before his family could get plane tickets out of the country. What happened? It seems that this "eager" North Korean woman was a spy.

There were many warning signs the missionary should have noticed. First of all, no North Korean refugees come to China talking negatively about their government, nor would they even know who Bill Clinton was. This missionary, in his zeal, overlooked these warning signs. Instead of helping a poor refugee, he was cheated of a lot of money that was then sent to the regime. When he ran out of money "helping" this lady, she turned in all the members she knew about. By telling stories of her starving family and friends and how she could help them, she milked the missionary of thousands of dollars, then had all of his contacts arrested.

Chinese missionaries don't have this problem. North Koreans know that Chinese Christians are poor and survive on very little. Because of this fact, the chances of a North Korean spy trying to get money from Chinese Christians are slim. The Chinese House Church has had to operate in secret and avoid infiltration by security bureau spies for decades. They are adept at knowing when someone is sincere, and when someone is trying to infiltrate their ranks. They know what it means to be "wise as serpents and innocent as doves." When the Chinese Christians face problems while working with North Koreans, it is normally due to security issues caused by foreigners who think they know it all and are more experienced than their Chinese brothers and sisters.

The North Koreans are aware of the Chinese efforts and are trying to stop them in any way they can, but it is virtually impossible. The Chinese are the only ones bringing in much needed investment and the needed experts for their desire for advancement. The Chinese are also propping up the North Korean government and keeping it from absolute collapse.

More than 50 years ago, the Chinese came to North Korea and helped suppress the Korean people with the anvil of communism and fight off the Americans. However, today, they are returning to help lift the weight of oppression and to share the Light of the World to the people trapped in the land of darkness. The "Reds" have indeed returned, but it's a different banner they are waving today... it is the banner of Jesus Christ.

9

FROM ASHES TO BEAUTY

How many Christians are in North Korea today? It is impossible to say for certain. A 2007 *Newsweek* article entitled "Prayer in Pyongyang" states, "estimates range from the low tens of thousands to 100,000." If that is true, it means that the Christian population in North Korea today is a fraction of a percentage point, while South Korea is estimated to be between 25% and 40% Christian and is considered to be the most Christian nation in Asia, after the Philippines. The same *Newsweek* article estimates that up to 5 million believers fled from North Korea to the South at the beginning of the Korean War.

Regardless of the exact number, we know for certain that the North Korean church is growing day by day. They have also developed clever and unique ways to practice their faith without attracting attention from the government—or even their neighbors. Though many of the extreme measures they must take create very untraditional churches with very little semblance to the megachurches with their choir robes, million-dollar sound systems, and ATMs in the South, we should remember that worship services in the 1st century were also held in homes without most of the things we associate with a "church."

Believers in North Korea are known to rip their Bibles up into small sections and hide them in secret places with each section hidden in a different location. If the police find any one of these torn-out portions, the others are still safely scattered around the area.

When a Christian wants to have a focused time of prayer, they must either go out to a deserted place in the wilderness, where there is no possibility of anyone seeing them, or at home they must bury themselves under their blankets so no one can hear their whispers of heartfelt prayer to God.

As strange as it may sound, there are even some reports of church services taking place by mobile phone! The mobile phones are smuggled into the country by North Koreans who go into China to look for food and supplies, but return as born-again Christians. The North Koreans will have a group of four or five people in a room close to the border where they can get reception. Sermons are delivered in less than ten minutes. Afterward there is prayer for the sick and even an altar call for those who might be present that might not fully believe! The North Korean government is now known to use GPS trackers to find these phones, but if the message is short enough, the conversation can be stopped before the church is discovered.

When it comes to corporate worship and church issues like tithing, one missionary said:

Due to the situation in North Korea, it's not possible for people to gather together on Sundays to worship. In other areas when people worshipped together they all got caught within a night. In one situation, a young man went to China, believed in Jesus, returned to North Korea, and evangelized his friends. After they met together to pray, all of them suddenly disappeared. This kind of thing doesn't just happen occasionally in a few areas, so worship is done quietly with two people or one family.

When they asked how they could tithe, I told them to always give one tenth of what they'd received from God to the poorest people after praying. God worked. There were people who gave pumpkins to others who then planted the seeds and gave the new pumpkins back to the first giver with many thanks.

Since it is impossible to sing Christian songs out loud, these small household churches of at most five people can only quietly read the hymns when they worship.

Believers in this situation have been known to memorize large portions of the Bible. One missionary who is familiar with the area said:

> I went from village to village preaching the Gospel. I wasn't allowed to travel, so I did most of my movement at night. The believers would eagerly receive me and listen intently to my teachings. There would only be three or four people at a time in our meetings. They were not allowed to have Bibles, so there was usually a loose board on the floor or a loose brick in the wall or foundation that partial Scripture could be hidden in. When it came time to pray or meet, the Scriptures would be pulled out of the secret hiding place with the utmost care. After some time, there would be no need to pull out the Scripture because every word would have been memorized.

A story in *The Washington Post* was run in April of 2001 that cited a story reported by the US State Department about a man and his wife who escaped North Korea. They were Christians and talked about the church's state at the turn of the century. They described the life of Christians there around the time of their escape in 1997. They asked that their names not be given because they still have family members living inside who would be punished if their identities were made public.

The Christian couple escaped to China with their son, who was later caught and thrown in prison. The family knows that their son's fate has been all but sealed. The mother said:

> My mother taught me the Ten Commandments, and we memorized hymns. Of course, we could never keep a Bible in the house. The [Communist] Party would regularly raid the house and go through all the belongings, looking for foreign books. If they found a Bible, you could be executed. My mother always told me although I could not show my belief in God, I must keep it inside.

The family only knew a few other Christians. One day the father was talking to his best friend and having a heart-to-heart when he learned that he too was a Christian. They were so excited. They were best friends for decades and it was not until he was 60 years old that he learned his dear friend was also a believer! He recalled how they would study the Bible together in secret, "He would listen to a Christian radio program broadcast from South Korea. He would make notes and hide them in his hat and come to my house. We had to do it in secret."

Below is the testimony of an underground Christian who witnessed the Communist takeover of North Korea and tells what it was like growing up as a Christian in that hostile environment:

> I was a young lady, twelve years old, when I believed in Jesus. My parents were Christians. Prior to the War of Southern Aggression [Communist name for the Korean War], there were many Christians in Chosun. Due to per-

secution during the Korean War and after, most of them fled to South Korea. In 1954, I was 12 years old. Many Christians began to disappear. There was once a Church building in my town but it was dismantled in 1954. Its deacons and pastor disappeared.

During school, teachers asked students to turn in any black books they may find in their homes. They were promised money. Some students did this, but later their families were not seen. It was told they moved, but since we were not allowed to move, we knew the Security Bureau was responsible.

My family kept our Bible. For three years, I memorized as much as I could. My father said I would need it, because one day our Bible may be found. Persecution of Christians became so bad that my father disposed of our Bible for the safety of our family. I did not know that would be the last time I would see a Bible for almost 50 years.

My parents both died of tuberculosis when I was 17. I did not know of any other Christians after their death. I had heard rumors of even family members turning each other in for being Christians.

I recited the parts of the Bible I remembered in my mind every day. I had remembered the book of Mark and First Timothy, as well as many Psalms. They would be my only hope for years.

Things in my country got worse and worse. After being raised by an uncle, and made to work in the fields by the government, my life was ok... until the famines.

By the time I was in my fifties—I forget the exact year— famine became worse and worse. I was raising my cousin's two daughters. She and her husband had died of complications from not having enough food. The children were about to starve to death, so I began going to China illegally to find food and bring it back.

This secret route I established during these times proved vital. By sharing the food I was retrieving from China with the border guards, I was allowed to cross without trouble.

In 2004, my age and health were no longer allowing me to be able to continue to make the trip. I found a permanent place to hide in China, in a small one-room shack with a coal heater.

One day, in 2006, I was told by a friend that was helping me that a pastor was coming to meet me. I was so excited. I had a few RMB saved, so I bought extra coal so it would be warm. I was amazed that the pastor came, and brought to me, a BIBLE! For the first time since I was a young girl, I had the Word of God. I wept and wept. The pastor told me that Chinese Christians had provided the Bible.

My eyesight was so bad, I could barely read it, but I was excited. God gave me a clear vision of how I could help my people once again. I began witnessing to North Koreans hiding in China. Many began to be saved. Some even wanted to go back to their villages.

I began to receive Bibles in audio format. I was told they were part of the Chinese Christians' way of reaching North Koreans. I was excited because many of the people I was helping couldn't read due to eyesight problems. I began helping deliver these to North Koreans in China. Many of them were saved. Some even started finding ways to help these audio Bibles get into Chosun. I know of over 100 North Koreans who have been saved because of these audio Bibles.

My health has become worse. I cannot receive medical

treatment in China, or I will be turned in to the authorities and sent back to Chosun. Next week I will be taken to Laos and then Thailand by Christian operatives working in China. Once in Thailand, I will be jailed for illegal entry, but later released and sent to freedom in South Korea, where it has been arranged for me to receive medical treatment for my tuberculosis. I regret having to leave, and would rather give my life for this sake, but I am too contagious to be of help without endangering others. I am only glad that I have been used of the Lord after having to be a secret Christian so long.

Chae, Ok Young

February 25, 2011

A Chinese missionary describes the abject poverty and hunger of the people she ministered to:

The [North Korean] women I met wore only tattered rags and didn't even have underwear. The clothes they had on were so tattered that I had to put them in a plastic bag and throw them away. When I took them to the bath house, it was the first time they had ever been to one and didn't even know how to wash themselves. As I washed them, lice and dead skin fell down like rain.

After a week, they started to be back in their right minds. They had been starving for so long that preaching to them didn't work... [In North Korea] they don't have pork or even rice to eat. Even the corn they eat is only the cob ground into powder and made into gruel... After thoroughly washing them, giving them new sets of clothes, and three meals a day, their bodies gradually recovered. When they asked, "Why do you help in this way someone you don't even know?" I began to preach to them, saying upfront that it was the love of God and God is truly alive. When the gospel is preached to North Korean refugees that way, they understand quickly because of the Juche ideology in North Korea. If you take out Kim Jong Il's name and put in God it fits perfectly.

Through this type of ministry, hundreds, if not thousands of North Koreans have met the Lord in China and returned to their hometowns to proclaim the Good News.

Chinese missionaries have also been able to evangelize inside North Korea, but they must be very careful in how they do so, as the following account explains:

Because you can't openly preach the gospel, every night between 12 and 5 am I would visit door to door while the children were sleeping. They would draw the curtains, tear a bit of cotton from an old blanket, soak it in cooking oil I had brought from China, and light it [because they had no candles or electricity]. Because I was so vexed I beat my breast and cried, "You are spiritually and physically starving, why don't you believe in Jesus? Believe in Jesus!" The husband then asked me to be quiet because it would be bad if the neighbors heard.

Their first reaction was to deny and ask, "Where is Jesus? Where is God?" But God was working and they listened quietly to me until 5am and that morning went out to walk with me and my disciples who kept preaching to them. (In North Korea you walk a lot because there aren't any cars. Five or six people always walk together because it is a place where you can be caught and eaten [by other people].) While we were walking, they asked me, "*Teacher, can we receive Jesus now?*"

In those situations, the others would keep watch while we went into a ditch in a field or deep into a forest where we would hold hands and I would lead them in a sinner's prayer. Like that, we would just lead them in a prayer and go back [to China], but later when we met, they would have memorized all the Bible verses [we had given them] and could pray very well. As the Bible says, we would just plant the seeds but God alone would yield the produce.

On top of the dangers, missionaries in North Korea also have to deal with those stubborn cases of rejection where only intense prayer seems to affect the situation. One missionary was invited to spend the night at the home of a schoolteacher and the following took place:

She said, "Where is God? Show me. If you show me, I'll believe. Thanks to the Great Leader Kim Il Sung we live like this, but where is God? Do you think you're helping by just giving us a little rice [in comparison to what Kim Il Sung gives us]?" Because she so stubbornly refused to believe in Jesus, I started to fast in that house from that day for one week and prayed, "Lord, help her to see you and know you!"

In North Korea, the food doesn't have any nutrients, so if someone fasts for even one day, they will die. I saw it many times. But even on the seventh day of the fast, she still slandered me.

In North Korea there is no place where you can weep loudly in prayer. At that time God gave me wisdom. The security officers never follow you to the graves and there, it is very normal for people to weep loudly, so I told my disciple to take me to his parent's grave. On the seventh day of the fast, I climbed with all my strength up the steep mountain, grabbing on to every little plant while praying, "Lord, please show yourself to her!"

While coming down the mountain I was full of joy and got to the house so quickly it felt like I had flown down the mountain. When I arrived at the house, I should have been dead, but I entered the house full of joy and smiling. The woman fell on her knees before me and said, "Teacher, I was wrong. God lives. Lead me in prayer." Just like that, we held hands, sobbed, prayed together, and started studying the Bible.

Sometimes the stories don't turn out as we'd like them to, but must submit everything to God's will and remember that He is in control. Love is generally something completely foreign to North Koreans—even the love between husband and wife or mother and child—which is something that often leads to tragic results:

One disciple had a plan to go to South Korea, but he gave up and continually brought Bibles and evangelical materials over [to North Korea], saying, "If I'm not there, who's going to do this?" He continued carrying materials until he was captured for good. He had been caught previously and sent on a spy mission to find me. (In this way those who are detained a few times are sent by the government as bait to spy.) That time I said to him, "I don't care what kind of mission you have, but when you're here you need to nurture yourself well, learn the Bible correctly, pray together, and after that do whatever you're supposed to do because if I die, I'm going to heaven."

After one month, he returned to North Korea and confessed to his wife that he hadn't accomplished his mission. She in turn reported him to the Security Bureau which gave him a three-year sentence. His wife also went out to China and I treated her very well and preached the gospel to her, but she was a spy. This kind of family isn't unusual. There are many cases of wives reporting their husbands to the security bureau.

When last we left off the story of "Mr. Lee" he was faithfully bringing Christian materials into North Korea and the Lord was using him mightily. Unfortunately, spies working on both sides of the border were able to figure out his route.

A spy posing as a North Korean refugee in search of food encountered some South Korean missionaries. From that contact, she was able to contact an American missionary. The American missionary, convinced that this spy had become a true believer, exposed her to many things that were going on from the China side of the border. This spy gathered information on routes for Bibles to go into the country from China, and routes that North Koreans were taking to leave the country. Mr. Lee became one of the first victims.

Mr. Lee, while coming out of North Korea to China, was shot by North Korean border guards. The gentleman he was traveling with was shot as well. Neither wound was fatal. They managed to make it to the China side of the river, and place a phone call to their familiar contact, informing them of what had happened, and begging for assistance. Someone had tipped off the North Koreans as to when and where Mr. Lee and his friend would cross.

After making the phone call, Chinese police immediately arrived at the scene. Both men, having been shot in the leg, could not run and were captured. Their cell phones were confiscated as well.

By the grace of God, the Chinese Christian that was on the way to help them arrived after the police and was able to avoid capture. The police, now knowing who the contact was in China, began a search. They arrested the contact's brother and retrieved contact information about several missionaries from him, but only after an extended period of intense interrogation.

Police began showing up at missionaries' houses the next night. Two South Korean missionaries had their visas revoked and were sent out of the country. An American missionary, having been tipped off, fled the country until things settled down and came back through a different port of entry.

The Chinese contact, who had been responsible for hundreds of Bibles going into North Korea, taking care of hundreds of North Korean refugee children, and providing food for Christians in North Korea, had to be spirited away at night. This worker, who had survived being jailed both in North Korea and China for preaching the gospel, had their entire ministry stripped from them due to the foolishness of one foreigner.

A friend with major ties to government officials in the region where the two captured North Koreans were being held was able to obtain the release of one of them. That brother was then taken by Chinese operatives to the border of another Asian country next to China and sent over. Once there, he got medical aid for his gunshot wound, recovered, and eventually was taken to South Korea, where he obtained freedom. Mr. Lee was not so fortunate.

The last that was heard of Mr. Lee was that he had been transferred to a North Korean prison. Since this incident, the gentleman that tried to help with his release has gone missing and has not been seen since October of 2010. The cost of discipleship is often very high and we thank the Lord for people like Mr. Lee and the Back to Jerusalem missionaries who are willing to pay that price.

Communist regimes and governments in general, have gone to great lengths to try to get people to behave. Despite the fact that stealing and killing another person's animal is a capital offence in North Korea, theft is still common. One family realized that the solution is Jesus Christ:

> The daughter of one family escaped to China, met me, and believed in Jesus. I told her that when she went back, she needed to evangelize her parents and I would come to them. Of course her parents didn't believe. Thievery is daily life for the people there, so I told them to never steal. "A child of God never steals, but God provides. The God who works in China, in South Korea, and in the Bible is the same God who works in this land, house, and you. The problem is, do you really believe or not." I coerced the parents to pray and said, "Pray and be prepared so that even if you starve to death, you die before God. A child of God is not a thief." Then I went back to China.
>
> After a while I returned to the same area. The daughter's mother held my neck and sobbed, saying, "We were starving for two days but didn't steal even once. We prayed, 'God please don't let us steal and don't let us die. Help us!' then you came with this truckload of things." I saw that if [North Koreans] truly received the gospel, they lived Biblically.

On another occasion, a missionary recalls the time that a North Korean woman's pigs caught a disease. She called the missionary, crying because the pigs were so sick that they were about to die. The missionary then prayed over the phone and told her to lay hands on each pig and pray for them. All the pigs survived.

The following account gives a good picture of what average North Koreans do to survive from day to day:

> In North Korea, the women make whiskey out of soybean waste, then the leftover waste from that process is fed to the pigs and the whiskey is sold to buy corn. One handful of corn can then be sold to buy enough corncob-flour noodles for three meals. This is the type of household commerce that women are involved in.
>
> All men without exception are obligated to work at jobs such as farms and coal mines without receiving pay. [Thus it is the women who feed the family.]

It is common knowledge that many South Korean Christians are praying for North Korea to open, be liberated, but did anyone ever think that North Koreans might be praying for not just their southern brothers and sisters, but the whole world as well?

> Those who believe in Jesus in that land have a faith that isn't polluted, but very pure and simple. Believers of Jesus in North Korea pray for South Koreans. [Whenever I'd bring supplies to them I would say,] "Believers from all over the world have sent these things to you. I am just the messenger. These things are not mine but are all sent by God. Because of that you must pray for those people! When you eat and use these things you need to pray!"

10

THE CHALLENGE OF JUCHE

O n June 15, 2009, Ri Hyon Ok, a 33-year-old mother of three was executed for distributing Bibles in North Korea. Three children had their mother taken from them just because she handed out some books! Even if you are not a Christian and view the Bible as a book of ignorance, is it worth taking someone's life? The repressive North Korean government was not satisfied with exterminating the life of this poor mother. They sent Ri's entire family, including her three children, to a prison camp.

Ri, a confirmed Christian, was executed in the northwestern city of Ryongchon, near the Chinese border. The most conservative estimates say there are more than 30,000 Christians in North Korea, but according to the U.S. government there are more than 6,000 Christians imprisoned in "Prison No. 15" alone. According to numerous eyewitness accounts, Christians receive much more torture than other inmates at these camps.

Christians are one of the most persecuted groups of people around the world. They are persecuted in China, India, Iran, Saudi Arabia, to name but a few. With all of this global persecution of Christians, what makes North Korea so special?

North Korea is continually ranked as the most oppressive country in the world for Christians and in many ways it is in a league of its own. In North Korea, Christians are not just merely killed, they are sent to death camps and gulags, run over with steamrollers, sodomized with foreign objects, forced to watch the murder of their loved ones, forced to abort their children, and executed by firing squads.

Kim Il Sung himself said, "Anti-government behavior and enemies of the state must be annihilated to the third generation." This murderous principle is applied rigorously to those considered a threat to the government—especially Christians.

In order to truly understand the insanity that defines North Korea and it's leaders and to gain insight into the source of their cruel behavior toward Christians, it is absolutely necessary to understand the national religion - Juche.

Juche—usually translated "self-reliance"—has been described (by those that understand it) as the world's fifth largest religion with more adherents than Judaism. Its mirror image to Christianity is uncanny.

Juche even has a perverted form of the Trinity – Father (Kim Il Sung), Son (Kim Jong Il), and the Spirit of the People (represented by a torch).

Juche has its own holy books, the speeches and writings of Kim Il Sung, which are revered and studied like the Bible is, in Christianity. School children are forced to memorize entire sections of these writings and recite them.

Juche has its own priests and clergy members, political officers who are assigned to schools and workplaces where they disciple the people in the ways of Juche. They too conduct confessionals. North Koreans perform self-criticism to report anything that they may have done throughout the week that may have been a "sin" against the government. Along with their meditations on "scripture," they write these confessions down in a red book called a "life planner" (a twisted version of a prayer journal). Juche also has songs for worship based on old

Christian hymns with altered lyrics.

Juche even has its own calendar! Since Kim Jong Il took power in 1997, the North Korean government has been dating documents based on the year of Kim Il Sung's birth (April 15, 1912). To North Koreans, 2011 is the year "Juche 100."

Juche has its own share of miracles as well. When a family is hungry, they pray to Kim Il Sung. When soldiers need strength in battle, they pray to Kim Il Sung. Children are even taught to bow in gratitude to portraits of Kim Il Sung and his ruling son when entering class and even at mealtimes.

Juche teaches that Kim Il Sung is an "eternal" president and when North Koreans die, they will be reunited with him and he will continue to live forever in the hearts and minds of the people. For them, eternal life means becoming part of the history of Juche and contributing to the great revolutionary struggle.

Driving through the countryside in North Korea, around afternoon break time, you can usually see farmers gathering in the fields or workers coming together into makeshift classrooms to do what they simply call, "study." A designated person (the Juche priest) will then pull out a book and begin reading from the writings of Kim Il Sung. After reading from a small segment, he will elaborate on it and explain it to the others. Much like an average sermon, the text will be read, an interpretation given, and applicable words of exhortation will follow. The meeting will end by singing songs of praise to Kim Il Sung. The "Great Leader" had undoubtedly learned much from his Christian upbringing, but unfortunately applied it to the worship of himself!

Juche is often explained as a socio-political ideology, but it is so much more than just ideology. It permeates all aspects of North Korean society. Juche requires North Koreans to bow down daily to two or three portraits, which must hang on the best wall in every home. The two main portraits are of Kim Il Sung and Kim Jong Il. Often, a portrait of Kim Jong Sook (Kim Jong Il's mother) is also used. Allowing these portraits to collect dust or in any way be damaged is a capital offence.

Folklore of brave North Koreans who risked their lives running into burning homes to save the "Kim" portraits are told and retold as acts of the highest valor.

There is very little doubt that Kim Il Sung's childhood experience in a Christian family had something to do with the formation of Juche. The experience of playing praise and worship music on the organ for church services must have made a strong impression on his mind. It is obvious that Kim used the same methods Christians employ to worship God and turned them around for his benefit. Watching a congregation adoring their Lord and Savior brings to mind stories of Satan desiring praise from the other angels.

Kim went around preaching atheism and regurgitating the words of Marxism-Leninism, but he recognized the power of Christianity and wanted it to be directed toward himself. It was actually a member of his staff, Hwang Jang Yop, who initially developed the ideology beyond its original implications. Hwang, often referred to as the architect of Juche, defected to the South in 1997, reportedly repented of his sins, and became a favorite speaker in South Korean churches until his death in 2010.

He claimed that Juche was originally meant for the people, following the humanist doctrine that "man is the master of everything and decides everything," but was hijacked to focus on worship of the regime. Juche has become a counterfeit Christianity, but lacks the power of the real thing. Because it lacks that power, the state of North Korea is deathly afraid of Christianity.

The North Korean government would challenge the idea of Juche being a religion. They would argue that it is the teaching of independence, free from the chains of capitalism. The idea was first introduced in 1955 to distance the people of North Korea from the control of the Soviet Union. Over time, Juche evolved by borrowing ideas and teachings from Marxism, Leninism, Mao, and Christianity. In 1972, Juche officially replaced Marxism-Leninism in the North Korean constitution. Juche attributes divine powers to the sole author, editor, and interpreter of Juche.

According to Juche, there is no god but Kim Il Sung. Even though he has been dead since 1994, he is still the "Eternal President" which means that North Korea is the only country in the world that is governed by a dead leader.

Juche teaches complete independence and the superiority of the Korean people, but nothing could be further from the truth. The ideology itself has made the people inferior and even a laughingstock to the rest of the world. Most of the food consumed in North Korea is provided by their most hated enemies: South Korea, Japan, and the "craven American dogs."

Juche has led to one major crop that they export: opium. Opium is North Korea's major export and continues to grow. This is not a private venture, but a state-sponsored enterprise. More than 98% of the factories in North Korea are not operating. There is a shortage of raw materials, electricity, fuel, and textiles needed for production. The customer base is simply not there. UN sanctions have taken their toll. The regime is desperate for money and drugs help them make up for losses.

Defectors who currently live in Seoul talk about working in the poppy fields as small children. They said that the boys would work for 40 minutes and the girls for 30. The workers would get too dizzy if they worked too long. Running drugs from North Korea is perfect because no one questions the government, thus it is considered legal (as they are considered the benefactors). According to U.S. Military intelligence officials in

Seoul, North Korea is the third-largest producer of opium. Estimates of drug revenue range from $100 million to $500 million per year!

The quality of North Korean drugs however is notoriously poor. Oftentimes, North Korean ships make money by transporting drugs from Myanmar where the quality is much higher. Myanmar is another country that is under tight control and has government-sponsored drug trade. Along with their illicit weapons trade, North Korea's drug trade has caused many countries to view their ships with suspicion.

Juche has not only provided the country with an independently sustainable drug trade, but has also led the nation to become one of the few places in the world with state-sponsored counterfeiting of U.S. money. In June of 2009, the U.S. Congress put out a report about the quality and quantity of the counterfeit money produced by North Korea. Most of this money finds its way to the border area of China.

The structure of Juche can actually be a bridge for the potential North Korean Christian. Everything is there. Even the songs of praise and worship are there, so long as the names God and Jesus replace the names of Kim Il Sung and Kim Jong Il. At the same time, this has also made it difficult for many North Koreans to worship God in Spirit and in truth. Quite often, North Korean defectors learn to merely parrot the songs and teachings in South Korean churches without actually having a personal relationship with the Lord—much in the same manner that they had blindly worshipped under the Juche model in their homeland.

The current regime is aware of the dangers that Christianity poses to their stronghold over the people and is willing to spare no expense to root it out and crush it completely. The government makes every effort to keep missionaries from having contact with North Koreans and vice versa. They implement every control known to man to keep their citizens from being exposed to the outside world. To an outsider, North Korean propaganda sounds completely ludicrous if not comical, but if this information was all that one heard day in and day out for a lifetime, there would be no way of knowing anything different. The authorities will do whatever is necessary to keep things that way.

A main way that they keep the masses from finding out about the outside world is simply through fear. The Korean War never ended for the North Koreans, so they are continually programmed to believe that much of the world, America in particular, is still out to occupy and enslave them the way it allegedly has the South.

On the right is a typical North Korean propaganda poster depicting Korean babies being killed by American soldiers.

Here is an example of the propaganda that is used in North Korea and can be found on the "Juche Girl" blog (mistakes are in the original):

I hate US because US come to Korea and throw babies inside the wells for Bush personal profit.

I told my brother that when I marry a good socialist comrade I want many children, for love of Dear Leader because I love Dear Leader more than everything.

My brother who is very smart praised me with a hug, but he warned me that in US, people are so poor that they can't have children of their own and they drown all the new babies all the time. I ask my brother who know everything what happen when people still want to not drown their baby and he reveal to me that Bush will send CIA spy to steal the people's babies against their will and put them on a big white US boat to sell them to Jews in Palestine country. I hate Bush.

That's why my brother says US is a country without love, or caring, unlike DPRK where all the comrades live for the love of Dear Leader who is the father of all Koreans. Then I asked how US can keep population if all babies are drown or sold away to Jews by Bush. He says that Bush send US GI inside Mexico country to steal all the babies there and make them into US without international knowing, which is why they are called illegal immigrants, so Bush can exploit them for slave labor in his secret salt mines on his ranch in Texas and that Bush also kidnaps Korean girls to make sex slave in White House. This scares me much and I can't sleep for fear of nightmare of Bush.

I hate Bush who drown and steal all the world babies for personal profit and make me have nightmares. I hold my picture of Dear Leader to my heart for comforting and I love Dear Leader very much."

Juche Girl's blog also teaches us about the prayers for the sick that are offered up to Kim Jong Il and Kim Il Sung.

This is what Juche Girl had to say about the picture above:

Bush oppresses the poor downtrodden people of the world for his own sick twisted pleasure. My brother showed me picture of Bush who pick up handicap people in wheelchair and toss them on the ground for laughing like maniac with the vampire Cheney.

Our Dear Leader would never do that. Dear Leader can make the handicap walk and the blind see. Dear Leader is always full of loving care for the people.

Once, our Dear Leader went to give guidance at the handicap hospital with one room full of people who had lost an arm or leg in accidents of construction sites, who were building a great powerful prosperous country. Dear Leader distributed arms and legs to those who needed arms and legs and when Dear Leader had finished distributing arms and legs all the people who had missing arms and legs did not miss one arm or leg any longer! Bush can't do that but Dear Leader can.

The Juche Girl blog expresses common beliefs espoused by most North Koreans. [The editor once met the child of a North Korean defector who had never met an American before. She stared at him confusedly for quite some time before asking her father in all seriousness, "Where are his horns and tail?"] Despite all this brainwashing, the regime knows that this delusional and fanatical adherence to Juche cannot continue if the people are exposed to the rest of the world and realize how poorly they fare compared to everyone else on the planet. If fear of the outside world isn't a big enough deterrent, they had to make sure that fear of the government would be.

In January 2003, MSNBC shared a testimony from a prison guard who was in charge of overseeing prisoners who had violated Juche principles. Ahn Myong Chol had worked at four different prisons and discussed with NBC News what he saw and did at those camps. Mr. Ahn said that many think that they would already be dead if they were not loyal to Kim Jong Il and Kim Il Sung. His testimony paints a picture of brutality akin to the Holocaust in 1940s Europe:

> They trained me not to treat the prisoners as human beings. If someone is against socialism, if someone tries to escape from prison, then kill him. If there's a record of killing any escapee, then the guard will be entitled to study in the college. Because of that, some guards kill innocent people. Beating and killing is an everyday affair.
>
> They are not treated as human beings; they are just like dogs or pigs.
>
> There is no instruction how to beat them, but the officers tell us to beat or kill them (the prisoners) without responsibility.

Ahn's testimony goes on to describe much of the killing and beating he witnessed while working in the camps. Among the least graphic events, he saw an older man beaten to death with an iron rod, people being beaten so severely that bone was exposed. Once two starving girls were kicked into a cesspool and drowned while trying to grab a discarded noodle from it.

Ahn describes how practically every bit of unfarmed land near the prison was full of graves. They would often discover buried bodies while cutting down trees and farmers would find bodies and bones when starting to farm a new area. Whenever an inmate died, the guards strictly forbade crying or any signs of mourning, saying, "The anti-revolutionary has died, so there is no reason to cry."

On top of the indiscriminate killings, rape of inmates is also the norm in these camps:

> A food factory produced soy sauce and cookies and bean paste. And here the women [who] worked were between 20 and 30 years old. The women are the sexual slaves of the security officers, they are forced to wear only white thin gowns and no underwear; they are not given underwear. They make all the beautiful women work here.

It is bad enough that people are put in these camps merely for questioning the government (or just being accused of doing so). The truth is that most inmates aren't even the alleged anti-revolutionaries, but are completely innocent families. Under Kim Il Sung's policy, all family members of a convicted criminal up to the third generation are punished. Ahn says, "The prisoners are imprisoned not because of their own guilt but because they are distant relatives, other family members are imprisoned as well."

There are two different types of prisons. One is meant

for brainwashing people in Juche ideology and the other for slavery and death. The first type is for political prisoners who have a chance of being reformed. Most Christians however are considered to be beyond all hope of re-education and are sent to the latter. Mr. Ahn worked at both types of prisons. He was working as a prison guard in the early 1990s when Amnesty International publicly criticized Pyongyang Songwori Prison. This brought a lot of international attention to the situation and forced North Korea to act.

North Korea decided to combine several prisons to prevent the international community from knowing which camps were "re-education centers" and which were death camps. They quickly merged Kaechon No. 14 and Hannam No. 15, as well as Hoeryong No. 22 and Hasung No. 16 with Chongjin No. 25. All of the furnishings and materials that could be transported were and then the vacant facilities were destroyed to remove all evidence of the slaughter that had taken place.

Much of the farm produce is provided by the work of prisoners, as well as things like coal, so closing several prisons had a big impact on the economy. To add to the stress of working at these prisons, the prison guards were also required to participate in Juche's self-criticism sessions. This aspect is very much like a Catholic confessional where the sins are confessed to a priest. The sessions are usually held about once a week and last about an hour, depending on what the person needs to confess. This self-judgment hour starts off with readings from Kim Il Sung's teachings. After the reading, they spend time reflecting on what they have done wrong during the week or anything that they may have witnessed that was against Juche. This is one of the most important control measures of the communal system. It keeps everything out in the open so that anything security forces may have missed is sure to be confessed either by the perpetrator or an informant who tells on them.

This adds to the amazing control mechanism that is in place in North Korea.

Once they finish confessing they must repent to the Great Leader. Ahn said, "If I don't say Great Leader then I will be punished. So I have to behave, otherwise all of my family members will be put in prison."

Juche is indeed a barrier that is difficult to get through, but the power of the Lord is still able to reach people in the middle of North Korea because the god of Juche is dead, but Jesus is alive! Christians in North Korea are quickly learning that there are many prayers that Kim Il Sung is not able to answer and that the ones he allegedly did answer, are lies. He is dead and has been for many years. How ironic it is to think that one day, when the true Savior and King of Kings returns, every knee will bow and every tongue will confess Him as Lord—even the likes of Kim Jong Il and Kim Il Sung who dedicated their lives to stealing the worship due Him.

11

FLIES IN THE OINTMENT

T he contents of this chapter must be prefaced by the statement that the authors have no desire to slander or defame anyone in any way, thus names are not used for those mentioned. Our purpose is only to give the side of the story that the media never covers when misguided foreigners do stupid things to try to "help" North Koreans.

On Christmas Day of 2010, an American political activist illegally crossed the border into North Korea from China, shouting to the North Koreans, and carrying a letter that urged Kim Jong Il to step down and free all political prisoners. He claimed he was acting on what God had told him to do, but his actions and the outcome of the situation may indicate otherwise. Everyone needs to evaluate the situation for themselves.

This man was NOT a missionary, nor did he live in China as many newspapers reported. Although he did make a couple of short trips to Yanji, China, he in fact resided in Seoul, South Korea. After he recklessly crossed into North Korea, several South Korean long-term missionaries in China were expelled. Although they were in no way connected to this activist, they came under suspicion due to the attention he brought to the region.

This is a major problem around the world. Motivated Christians with great intentions and a burning desire to serve want to make a difference and jump feet first into the lion's den without considering the language, culture, laws, and current workers on the field in those areas. Oftentimes, they give very little thought about the consequences of their actions and how it might impact others. In this situation, one independent act of political activism by someone claiming to be on a mission from God brought several long-term missionaries' ministries to a screeching halt. Westerners, Americans in particular, need to understand that not everything is about them individually and they are not the only ones who suffer for their actions.

Due to the attention brought to the region by this man, several foreigners also lost their visas to enter North Korea. These foreigners had been working for a long time to establish themselves in the country for the sake of the Lord's work, and lost their hard-earned foothold overnight due to one political activist's foolishness.

People need to realize that when Chinese and North Korean officials loose face, the local population suffers. Due to the small amount of media attention this man drew toward China, the local government took action. The officials in the area where he illegally crossed into North Korea immediately went on a manhunt for North Korean refugees. Of course the local Chinese authorities knew exactly where to go to find them. The situation is comparable to the drug trade in some corrupt metropolitan cities. The drug dealers are out on the streets everyday dealing drugs while the police turn a blind eye. They know who the dealers are and where they operate, but for the most part don't give them too much grief. Even when gang violence takes a few casualties, not too much of a stir is caused. However, if a little girl is shot over a drug deal gone bad and that story makes it to the international news, then a great deal of pressure will come down on the leadership of the city and a manhunt for every drug dealer will begin. The police will know exactly who to search for, where to go, and in which areas to find them.

The situation is the same in China. The North Koreans— considered to be illegal economic migrants by the authorities despite their rightful status as refugees, did not cause a lot of trouble. The police found it easier just to crack down on those who became too apparent. However, once Beijing was alerted about large numbers of foreigners and refugees living in the border area and that foreigners there were engaged in illegal activities supporting North Koreans, the hammer came down hard and the police had to 'skin some hide' to prove to the central government that they were cracking down.

Beyond just the expulsion of missionaries, what is truly sickening is that because of what this activist did, over 100 North Korean refugees hiding in China were rounded up and repatriated to North Korea—many to their deaths. Over 50 North Korean children were left as homeless orphans in China as their moms were caught, thrown on the ground like rag dolls, tied, and shipped to North Korea for punishment. These children will never see their mothers again...all because someone wanted to play hero. Unlike this man who got to go back home to much sympathy and cheers, those writing this book were left to clean up the mess he left behind. This is what took place on the China side of the river.

On the North Korean side, many border guards were replaced by Security Bureau personnel as their government tightened security as well. This may not seem like a big change to those not familiar with the situation, but the truth is that it made a big difference.

A system of survival was in place for the border region of China and North Korea. Many North Koreans had made deals with border guards to allow them to slip into China to find food for their villages. In turn, these border guards were given a portion of the goods that the North Koreans were able to bring back, such as food, clothing, and money. Many North Koreans were shocked when they came to familiar guard posts, expecting to give the standard bribe to one of their cronies for exit into China, and instead were greeted by Security Bureau agents who arrested them and sent them to hard labor camps. Many villagers starved to death that winter because their long-standing way of being fed from China was immediately cut off.

North Korea is one of the most closed countries in the world to the gospel. There is NO freedom of religion. This was the reason why the activist said he was going into North Korea. He said that he wasn't coming out until every Christian had freedom. He didn't want any assistance from the U.S. government and he did not want the help of any former U.S. president.

The torture and the mind games that the North Koreans have perfected over the years cannot be underestimated. The torture that he undoubtedly received cannot be discussed lightly and most people in the same situation would have said whatever they needed to say in order to make the pain stop and the nightmare go away.

This man undoubtedly knew this but had never experienced it. He went trumpeting into North Korea with a letter demanding freedom for the North Koreans and thought he was prepared for whatever punishment would come, but it wasn't long before things changed. Once captured in North Korea, he confessed and repented in an official statement. It's not unusual for someone to buckle under the pressures of torture, but it is a serious issue when that person claims to be representing the Lord Jesus Christ while openly lying in order to save their skin. Here is the main part of his confession:

I trespassed on the border due to my wrong understanding of the DPRK caused by the false propaganda made by the West to tarnish its image. The West is massively feeding "Children of Secret State," "Seoul Train," and other documentary videos with stories about nonexistent "human rights abuses" and "mass killings" in the DPRK and "unbearable sufferings" of its Christians and the like.

This false propaganda prompted me, a Christian, to entertain a biased view of the DPRK...

... Upon trespassing on the border, I thought I would be either shot to death by soldiers or thrown behind bars, prompted by Americans' false propaganda about the DPRK. However, the moment I trespassed on the border, the attitude of soldiers toward the trespasser made me change my mind.

Not only service personnel but all those I met in the DPRK treated me in a kind and gentlemanly manner and protected my rights. I have never seen such kind and generous people...

... Another shocking fact I experienced during my stay in the DPRK is that the religious freedom is fully ensured in the DPRK, a reality different from what is claimed by the West. Being a devout Christian, I thought such things as praying are unimaginable in the DPRK due to the suppression of religion.

I, however, gradually became aware that I was wrong. Everybody neither regarded praying as something unusual nor disturbed it. I was provided with conditions for praying everyday as I wished. What astonished me more was that a Bible was returned to me.

This fact alone convinced me that the religious freedom

is fully ensured in the DPRK.

I came to have stronger belief as I had an opportunity to attend the service in the Pongsu Church in Pyongyang. I worshipped there. There was the Jondosa [assistant pastor] there, there was a pastor, there was a choir, they knew the hymns, they knew the word of God. That's why I was completely amazed. But I began to weep and weep in the Christian service because I learned that there are churches and Christians such as Pongsu Kyohoe (Church) in different cities and regions all throughout the DPRK. They worship, pray and preach freely the word of the Bible and Christ word. I've learned that in the DPRK people can read and believe whatever they want, whenever they want, wherever they want, that there's complete religious freedom for all people everywhere throughout the DPRK.

What I have seen and heard in the DPRK convinced me that I misunderstood it. So I seriously repented of the wrong I committed, taken in by the West's false propaganda.

I would not have committed such crime if I had known that the DPRK respects the rights of all the people and guarantees their freedom and they enjoy a happy and stable life.

I have felt shock, embarrassment and shame. Here, I'm in the lands where people respect human rights. Not just respecting human rights. They have actually loved me and showed me more than just human rights. They have shown me grace. I repent and ask for the forgiveness of the DPRK, for my misunderstanding totally, DPRK's reality and my illegal behavior. Had I known the reality of the DPRK, what I've learned here, what I have been shown here, what I've been taught here, what I've been informed here by all the kind people here about the DPRK, I would have never done what I did on the December 25th and I repent and I'm very sorry. (*Viewed on KCNA News*).

Of course, after his release, this man changed his story. For a while he kept silent and was so mentally distraught that he even attempted suicide (a very un-Christian thing to do). Eventually he became a political activist again, has been involved in more publicity stunts, and has released a statement saying he was sexually abused while in North Korea.

Only a month after his illegal entry into North Korea, a copycat entry by another American took place. This one went virtually unnoticed in the mainstream media, yet not unnoticed by Chinese officials. Once again, more refugees were rounded up. Most of them in this wave were "temporary" refugees; ones coming to China to seek food and medical care for their children. Once again, refugees were caught, sent back to North Korea, and imprisoned in labor camps. Once again, children were left homeless and without parents in North Korea.

Prior to both of these illegal entries into North Korea, there was the case of the two journalists from Current TV. A quick reading of their book and one can quickly become confused and appalled at the seemingly bogus story.

These journalists were supposedly "abducted" in China by North Koreans in March of 2009. While it is a known fact that abductions are commonplace in the border region, this was NOT the case with these journalists. They were arrested after they illegally entered North Korea, which can even happen in a free country.

These two reporters claim they were arrested, "on the border." There are multiple witnesses that have made it quite clear they were arrested after illegally entering North Korea.

A similar fate awaits anyone who illegally enters the borders of the United States. Try to illegally walk across any border in the world with video cameras and notepads and you will see a similar response, if not worse. Their "official story" was released to many news outlets:

Our guide, a Korean Chinese man who often worked for foreign journalists, had brought us to the Tumen River to document a well-used trafficking route and chronicle how the smuggling operations worked. There were no signs marking the international border, no fences, no barbed wire. But we knew our guide was taking us closer to the North Korean side of the river. As he walked, he began making deep, low hooting sounds, which we assumed was his way of making contact with North Korean border guards he knew. The previous night, he had called his associates in North Korea on a black cellphone he kept for that purpose, trying to arrange an interview for us. He was unsuccessful, but he could, he assured us, show us the no-man's land along the river, where smugglers pay off guards to move human traffic from one country to another.

When we set out, we had no intention of leaving China, but when our guide beckoned for us to follow him beyond the middle of the river, we did, eventually arriving at the riverbank on the North Korean side. He pointed out a small village in the distance where he told us that North Koreans waited in safe houses to be smuggled into China via a well-established network that has escorted tens of thousands across the porous border.

Feeling nervous about where we were, we quickly turned back toward China. Midway across the ice, we heard yelling. We looked back and saw two North Korean soldiers with rifles running toward us. Instinctively, we ran.

We were firmly back inside China when the soldiers apprehended us. Producer Mitch Koss and our guide were both able to outrun the border guards. We were not. We tried with all our might to cling to bushes, ground, anything that would keep us on Chinese soil, but we were no match for the determined soldiers. They violently dragged us back across the ice to North Korea and marched us to a nearby army base, where we were detained. Over the next 140 days, we were moved to Pyongyang, isolated from one another, repeatedly interrogated and eventually put on trial and sentenced to 12 years of hard labor.

Those who are familiar with that area can see many contradictions in this story. There are no signs marking the international border, yet they knew their guide was taking them closer to the North Korean side of the river. Anyone who can read a map would know where the border area is because there is a huge river there. The river is the border. They knew that, indicating that they knew the Tumen River and then at a later point said they felt nervous about where they were and turned back to China. They were fully aware that they were illegally going into North Korea. Later in their story they say they were in China when they were arrested. That is the part that seems a little confusing, because if they didn't know where the border was earlier (even though they were familiar with the Tumen River), how did they know they were in China then? And the guide leading the way into North Korea, with them following at a distance, got away, yet they didn't? Maybe they thought that North Korea treated people illegally entering North Korea the same way the U.S. does with its illegal entries: provide basic supplies like immediate hydration, food, food stamps, Medicaid, welfare, and citizenship to babies born within the borders (and even more if one enters through California).

The journalists appear on "The Oprah Winfrey Show", sign a big book deal, and seem to benefit from a bad situation. Meanwhile, North Koreans are still starving to death, have no religious freedom, and live in a country that still rates the worst in the world for human rights violations. Other than making money for the journalists, what did these actions accomplish? It cost a few hundred thousand dollars of US taxpayers' money to retrieve them, the lives of North Korean refugees and villagers killed in the crackdowns that followed, caused the loss of some longstanding gospel ministries, and increased difficulty for those actually trying to help North Koreans.

There are lives at stake here. In order to help the North Koreans there will have to be some brave people who are willing to stand up against the tyrannical dictatorship of Kim Jong Il. There are serious stakes involved and when that activist crossed the border, there were many missionaries that were praying for him. When the copycat entry took place, there were many people praying for him as well. When the journalists were brought home on a plane with former President Clinton, there were many families and Christian communities that rejoiced and gave thanks and praise to Jesus Christ.

However, there is a larger dilemma here that needs to be evaluated. How many days did the reporters spend in the area near North Korea before they were arrested? How many months did those activists spend personally reaching out and ministering to the people of North Korea? There are lives at stake and families that are ruined in the blink of an eye due to actions based on emotion or a desire to provide a good "story" for the media. Meanwhile, there are missionaries who have been working in North Korea for many years and have established ways and methods to truly help the people of North Korea.

There are missionaries providing rice, blankets, money, and most importantly, the gospel of Jesus Christ to the North Korean people today. These routes are not easy. The relationships needed for such opportunities are not easy to establish and are even harder to maintain. A missionary family can easily spend their entire life trying to set up a lifeline for the people in North Korea and in the blink of an eye see it washed away because of the acts of a zealous individual who has never lived in the area and will never return again.

It is not fair to pick out these few individuals and belittle them for their actions—this kind of thing has happened before with North Korea and will happen again—but these are the most recent events and people in the field are still suffering the consequences. There are communities in both China and North Korea that are angry. There is a huge mess that was made and those already overwhelmed with work on the ground are left to clean it up. Without exaggeration, many bridges were destroyed, many children have had their mothers dragged away, and in some cases, people lost their lives.

Missionaries are willing to—and often do—risk their lives for the gospel of Jesus Christ. They are willing to put the health and welfare of their families at risk to help the people that they are called to serve. They are willing to die on the mission field to represent the name of Jesus Christ, but they don't want to risk everything for the silly act of an activist who has sacrificed little more than a plane ticket and some time off work before being detained in North Korea and will bring no glory to the name of Jesus Christ.

CONCLUSION

N orth Korea is dark and a heavy weight hangs around the necks of its people and keeps them in bondage. It is hard to predict when there will be an end to the regime and a beginning to sweeping revival. It is possible they both may have already started. It is hard to say, even in the annals of history, where one ends and the other begins.

There is no way to know how to deal with the current leader. The international community has done everything to accommodate Kim Jong Il in order to obtain a guarantee of peace and stability on the peninsula. They have tried waiting on peace to come naturally, but there are few signs that patience will pay off. Many South Koreans placed all of their hope in the "Sunshine Policy" introduced by Kim Dae Jung which promised that understanding, compromise, patience, and dialog would bring the two sides together. They were wrong. The "Sunshine Policy" has completely failed. North Korea is not more open as a result and it seems that the policy only bought the regime much-needed time to conduct operations necessary to develop weapons of mass destruction and send more spies to further infiltrate South Korean society.

Large amounts of money and aid from the international

community have been used in attempts to lure the regime into reasonable dialog. Unfortunately those large donations were made with little to no oversight of how the aid and funds were distributed. In the end, the regime deprived the starving women and children of aid and directed all resources to the military. North Korea did not use their own money for aid, but rather used it to carry out clandestine operations to become a nuclear power.

Most of the world is starting to realize that North Korea may not be capable of ever opening up. Every agenda pursued to encourage North Korea to reform has been thwarted. Most leaders around the world now favor a tougher response to Pyongyang's unpredictable outbursts.

The world has watched with eager anticipation as Kim Jong Il was courted by the Chinese. China's role was to encourage North Korea to open special economic zones in order to allow direct foreign investment in their country—something highly advantageous to the Chinese. Tours in Guangzhou and Shanghai had been broadcast with much glee and expectation. Chinese officials were even quoted as saying that the Dear Leader "wanted one too" after visiting a Shanghai factory built in partnership with General Motors.

China has been offered many deals under the table to use their influence on North Korea to bring more transparency to the hermit nation. China's efforts are usually followed by momentary victories, but nothing that endures the test of time. After one tour in China, the North Korean regime supposedly acknowledged the need for economic change. The government newspaper *Rodong Shinmun* made a vague call for economic reform, improvement in technology, and expanding production, but nothing significant ever came of it.

One common billboard in Pyongyang shows a mother and child in front of a department store and declares, "We have reached a turning point." People have more reason to believe that now than ever before, as the regime has long promised prosperity for everyone by 2012—the 100th anniversary of the birth of Kim Il Sung.

Intelligence groups around the world report on this good news, news agencies in the international community take notice and become hopeful, and leaders of the free world take a deep breath thinking that they have bought an extra moment of peace for the world.

However, nothing could be further from reality. North Korea is just as closed today as it has ever been. In 2009, North Korea decided to change their currency and forced everyone to exchange their old notes for new ones, allowing each family to exchange a maximum of only $60 USD. Families with even modest savings lost everything above that small amount. It was a blatant attempt to reduce the entire population to an equal level of poverty. This made the financial disparity even more severe.

The situation is not going to get better in North Korea on its own. Politicians don't have a clue how to fix the situation. They don't know how to deal with Kim Jong Il. They are at a loss for an effective strategy. North Korea is one of the poorest countries in the world with the fewest resources, yet it seems that the leadership has completely out-foxed every high-priced consultant in the world. Billions of dollars have been spent to find ways to bring down the regime, obtain military intelligence, or get the regime to open up dialog in a meaning-ful way, but it has all been to no avail. The Preacher's words in Ecclesiastes couldn't be truer for international dealings with North Korea: "Vanity of vanities, all is vanity." It is all useless and every effort done without the Holy Spirit will be futile.

The only way to reach North Koreans or see a change in the country is through Spirit-led revival akin to that of China in the 1980's. The only way North Korea will have any chance of improvement is through the gospel of Jesus Christ being preached effectively within its borders.

Today missionaries are training on the border of Korea and are going in with every opportunity available. The government of North Korea cannot possibly stop them. The borders are becoming more and more vulnerable to the attacks of zealous missionaries. People are going in; Bibles are going in; projectors and training materials are going in; video players and even miniature audio players with the Word of God are penetrating those fortified borders with the unconquerable message of the eternal gospel.

The walls are coming down around North Korea because of the underground house churches that are slowly starting to rise. There is a genuine fear from the government, who is acutely aware of its inability to stop it. That is why their rule is absolute and their punishments so severe. The enemy knows that his time is limited.

The Light of the World is bringing in truth-bearers to set the captives free and no darkness can overcome it.

It is our hope that this book not only educates you about what is taking place in the country today and the history behind its current situation, but that you are also motivated as a reader to stand in prayer for your brothers and sisters in North Korea and become a partner with the Chinese House Church as they send in tools and people to reach the North Koreans with the gospel of Jesus Christ.

You can become a partner by logging on to:

www.backtojerusalem.com

You can also go to the Back to Jerusalem Facebook "Official Page," where daily updates are given about the progress of the Chinese Missionaries who are focused on taking the gospel into North Korea.

ACKNOWLEDGEMENTS

Thanks to MOGEE Photography for providing illustrations for the book.

Thank you to Brother Zhu for his dedication to making this book easier to read.

Thank you to Sandra Leow for bartering with us; editing of this book for a meal at McDonalds.

Special thanks to the underground Christians of North Korea who have risked their lives for the sake of the gospel. May God bless and protect them.

Thanks to the Back to Jerusalem missionaries that are willing to forsake all to reach North Korea with the gospel.